Andrew Woods

OXFORD GRAMMAR 5

T0342669

Name: _____

Class: _____

OXFORD
UNIVERSITY PRESS
AUSTRALIA & NEW ZEALAND

CONTENTS

OXFORD UNIVERSITY PRESS

TOPIC 4: SENTENCES, CLAUSES, CONJUNCTIONS, DIRECT AND INDIRECT SPEECH AND APOSTROPHES

TOPIC 5: USING GRAMMAR

TOPIC 6: ENRICHMENT

UNIT 1.1 — Common and abstract nouns

Noun Girl

When clever Cleo gets home from school on Wednesdays, she quickly grabs a bowl of instant noodles and hurries off to her bedroom to do her science homework.

For it is there that in the blink of an eye she transforms ...

She gains the brain strength of ten famous scientists.

She becomes more powerful than the invention of solar energy.

She is able to answer every question in seconds flat.

She thinks faster than a neutron collider.

She is able to use her fantastic brainpower to finish her homework before her noodles get cold.

Her brainpower makes her invincible, and in one intelligently worded sentence she can repel her little brother who dares to open her bedroom door.

Clever Cleo has become...

Noun Girl
(the name on everyone's lips!)

Use nouns to label the picture of Noun Girl.

OXFORD UNIVERSITY PRESS

Common nouns name people, things and places. For example: *car, woman, computer, book, chair*

1 Use the clues to write common nouns used in the description of Noun Girl and her powers.

a   Cleo can use an intelligently worded _____ to repel her brother.

b   Noun Girl has the strength of ten _____

c   This is the place where Cleo becomes Noun Girl. _____

d   Noun Girl thinks faster than a _____

e   Noun Girl uses her brain power to finish her _____

f   This is the amount of time that Noun Girl can answer every science question _____

Nouns that name feelings or qualities are called abstract nouns.

2 Write the abstract nouns from the box that best fit in the sentences.

> encouragement   wisdom   bravery   idea   pride   freedom

Abstract nouns name things that you cannot see or touch. For example: peace, excitement, horror

a   After saying some intelligent words to her little brother, Noun Girl was able to reach the _____ of her bedroom.

b   Our hero used her _____ to find out what a neutron collider is.

c   Noun Girl showed great _____ in rescuing the moth from the lamp light.

d   With _____ from herself, Noun Girl finishes her homework.

e   Cleo took great _____ in her Noun Girl costume.

f   Cleo's _____ was to dress up as a scientist to do her science homework.

3 Change these words to abstract nouns by adding the suffix -*ness*. (Take care with **j**, **k** and **l**.)

a   sad _____

b   kind _____

c   great _____

d   dark _____

e   selfish _____

f   clever _____

g   thankful _____

h   careless _____

i   willing _____

j   happy _____

k   lazy _____

l   lonely _____

4 Write the abstract nouns that can be formed from these adjectives.

a   beautiful _____

b   courageous _____

c   jealous _____

d   funny _____

e   strong _____

f   angry _____

CHALLENGE

On a separate piece of paper or on a computer, write or type a sentence containing at least one of these abstract nouns.

> joy   sorrow   fear   anger

Col's collector cards

Col has been busy collecting the new set of Collector's Collective Noun Cards. Here are some of the cards he has collected so far.

Card 12

a team of puppies

Card 19

a bouquet of thieves

Card 5

a gang of cattle

Card 27

a choir of flowers

Card 2

a forest of birds

Card 11

a flock of grapes

Card 15
a litter of footballers

Card 7

a bunch of singers

Card 3
a herd of trees

OXFORD UNIVERSITY PRESS

Collective nouns name groups of people or things that are similar. For example: *team, family, herd, bunch.*

1 As you can see on page 6, the printers have mixed up the captions on the nine Collective Noun Cards that Col has collected so far. Write the correct collective noun for each card.

a   Card 12 should be a _____ of puppies.

b   Card 19: a _____ of thieves.   c   Card 5: a _____ of cattle.

d   Card 27: a _____ of flowers.   e   Card 2: a _____ of birds.

f   Card 11: a _____ of grapes.   g   Card 15: a _____ of footballers.

h   Card 7: a _____ of singers.   i   Card 3: a _____ of trees.

2 Circle the best collective noun in each sentence.

a   The farmer moved his (bunch / crowd / herd) of cattle into the dairy.

b   The (crowd / flock / team) of spectators at the cricket final were asked to be patient.

c   The (army / troop / crew) of sailors struggled to maintain the (convoy / flock / swarm) of ships.

3 Match the collective nouns with the words in the box.

a   pride _____   b   convoy _____

c   band _____   d   gaggle _____

e   suite _____   f   string _____

g   library _____   h   bale _____

i   nest _____   j   punnet _____

geese	trucks
lions	musicians
beads	wool
eggs	strawberries
books	furniture

Common nouns name things, people or places. Common nouns only start with a capital letter if they begin a sentence. Here are some common nouns: *chair, bird, tree, card, puppy.*

4 Write three common nouns for each group.

a   Things that you might find in a kitchen _____

b   Things in a playground _____

c   Places where you could go for a swim _____

5 Most common nouns can be plurals. Write these common nouns as plurals.

a   flower _____   b   thief _____   c   puppy _____

d   potato _____   e   goose _____   f   bush _____

CHALLENGE

On a separate piece of paper or on a computer, write down or type what we are talking about when we refer to the following nouns.

a   battalion   b   galaxy   c   orchard   d   swarm

It's a laugh!

Simon's Pet Corner

What can I do for you today, Mrs Lewis?

I'd like that bird, please.

Polly is a very rare parrot and costs $500

Could you please send me the bill?

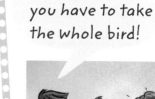

I'm sorry, but you have to take the whole bird!

Q. Where's Spiderman's home page?

A. On the worldwide web

Q. What do you call the small rivers that flow into the Nile?

A. Juveniles.

Q. What did the Pacific Ocean say to the Atlantic Ocean?

A. Nothing, it just waved.

Why was the boy from Egypt confused?

Because his daddy was a mummy

Baker Street School

Now, children, who, according to the Bible, was the first woman?

I'll give you a clue. Think of an apple.

Yes, Rupert.

Was it Granny Smith, Miss?

OXFORD UNIVERSITY PRESS

Proper nouns are special names for people, things or places. For example:

people	*Mary, Spiderman, Wonder Woman, Prime Minister*
things	*Grand Final Day, Yahtzee, Tuesday, Mitcham Primary School*
places	*Australia, Murray River, Pacific Ocean, Baker Street*

1 Find the proper nouns from the joke page that match these descriptions.

a   the name of the person wanting to buy the bird _____

b   the country where mummies are found _____

c   the name of the pet shop owner _____

d   the name given to a superhero _____

e   the name of a school _____

f   the name of a religious book _____

g   the name given to a river _____

h   the name given to a type of apple _____

i   a student at Baker Street School _____

j   the name of the parrot _____

2 Match the proper nouns in Box A with the common nouns in Box B.

a Captain Cook	b Pacific		
c American	d Barker Road		
e Ford Ranger	f April	**A**	
g *The Witches*	h Scott Morrison		
i Murray	j Sydney		

i ocean	ii address		
iii car	iv explorer		
v nationality	vi book	**B**	
vii month	viii river		
ix politician	x city		

Answers: _____

_____

CHALLENGE

Find proper nouns to name an example for each of the following.

a   A country beginning with **c**.   b   A river beginning with **n**.

c   A mountain beginning with **m**.   d   A planet beginning with **u**.

e   A book character whose name begins with **p**.   f   A make of car beginning with **h**.

Introducing the Dorgs

Here are some of the Dorgs.

Rosie is a sheep dog.

Rosie is a very clever sheep dog.

We can't help but be impressed by the way Rosie always gets it right!

Those sheep don't stand a chance with Rosie around.

Now, Ralph is a cattle dog. Like Rosie, Ralph is very clever and he always gets it right too.

With Ralph on the job at round-up time those cattle haven't got a chance!

Finally, there is good old Rex. Rex is a police dog. Rex isn't quite as clever as Rosie or Ralph but he is very enthusiastic, so...

...I don't think those police stand a chance either!

OXFORD UNIVERSITY PRESS

Some nouns have the same spelling whether singular or plural.
For example: *one sheep – a flock of sheep; the aircraft – many aircraft*

1 Write plural nouns from the box to match the clues.

a ANZAC = Australian and New Zealand Army _____

b We are freshwater fish related to salmon. _____

c We are sporting events such as running, jumping and throwing. _____

d We are pigs. _____

e We are large North American mammals related to elks. _____

moose

athletics

Corps

swine

trout

2 Unjumble these plural nouns using the clues in brackets to help you.

a f t a r c (boats, yachts, jet-skis) _____

b s h f i (water dwellers) _____

c d s u q i (tentacled sea creatures) _____

d e d e r (large mammals) _____

e o i l p e c (law enforcers) _____

f n s l m o a (type of fish) _____

g n i n i n s g (a team's turn to bat) _____

Remember: When you use plural nouns in your writing, the verb in the sentence must agree with the plural. For example: The cattle **are** in the paddock. NOT The cattle **is** in the paddock.

Some nouns are always in plural form. For example: *scissors, trousers, clothes, cattle*

3 Rewrite the following nouns correctly.

a tweezer _____ b scissor _____ c binocular _____

d trouser _____ e pyjama _____ f plier _____

Some words ending with **o** following a vowel just add **s** to form plural nouns. For example: *radios, rodeos*
Some words of foreign origin ending with **o** just add **s** to form plural nouns. For example: *kimonos, patios*
Some shortened words ending with **o** just add **s** to form plural nouns. For example: *photos, autos*

4 Rewrite the following as plural nouns.

a folio _____ b piano _____ c banjo _____

d kilo _____ e dynamo _____ f ratio _____

g tempo _____ h zoo _____ i tattoo _____

CHALLENGE

Read the comic strip on page 10 and, on a separate piece of paper, write down the three plural nouns and the rule they follow.

What's on the menu?

Son: What's for tea tonight, Mum?
What's in the pot?
I could eat a horse, Mum.
Tell me what we've got.

Mum: Toasted eggs and fish legs,
Chocolate stew.
Icky-sticky, black bread
And porridge like glue.
Mushy peas, banana skins,
A baked mud muffin.
Soggy ice-cream sandwiches
With Vegemite stuffin'!

Top it all off
If you want more
We've sweet and sour woolly grubs
On which to gnaw.
Then we have for afters
Feathers from a hen
So you see what's for tea, Son —

Son: Yeah! Casserole again!

OXFORD UNIVERSITY PRESS

Adjectives tell us more about nouns. For example: The **poor** mule struggled with the **heavy** load.

1 Use the poem to help you find adjectives that describe the following nouns.

a _____ stew   b _____ bread   c _____ peas

d _____ sandwiches   e _____ muffin   f _____ grubs

2 What do the following adjectives describe in the poem?

a glue-like _____   b hungry _____

c sweet and sour _____   d feathered _____

3 Circle the adjectives that have been used to describe the underlined nouns.

a The hen's **feathers** were fluffy.

b The **pot** was full of grubs.

c My **eggs** were toasted and my **muffins** were baked.

d "Thanks, Mum, **dinner** was delicious."

e The **sandwiches** were soggy.

f The **woolly grubs** were sweet and sour.

4 Match the adjectives in Box A with the nouns you think they best fit in Box B.

A

a shady _____

b fierce _____

c ancient _____

d slithery _____

e ripe _____

f comfortable _____

g stale _____

h shaggy _____

i delicious _____

B

meal

monument

bread

dog

tree

banana

serpent

tiger

armchair

Sometimes *adjectives* do not come before the noun they are describing. For example: The peas were mushy. The bread was black.

CHALLENGE

On a separate piece of paper or on a computer, use the letters of your first name to write or type adjectives that describe you.

For example: **P**eaceful **A**thletic **U**nusual **L**oving   **S**porty **A**rtistic **L**ighthearted **M**odest **A**gile

Dorgs again!

quick

quicker

quickest

strong

stronger

strongest

good

better

best

smart

smarter

smartest

OXFORD UNIVERSITY PRESS

Adjectives tell us more about nouns. Some adjectives are used to describe and compare characters.
When we compare some adjectives, just add *er* or *est*.
For example: *Rex is quick. Rosie is **quicker**. Ralph is **quickest**.*

1 Use the comic strip on page 14 to help you write adjectives to complete the following.

a Rex is strong. Rosie is _____. Ralph is _____.

b Rex is _____. Rosie is _____. Ralph is best.

c Rosie is smart. Ralph is _____. Rex is _____.

The spelling of some adjectives needs to be changed before adding *er* or *est*.
For example: *big, bigger, biggest   happy, happier, happiest*

2 Add *er* and *est* to the following adjectives. Read the rule first!

Rule: Double the last letter.

a hot _____   b thin _____

c sad _____   d fit _____

Rule: Change the *y* to *i*.

e funny _____   f heavy _____

g noisy _____   h pretty _____

Some adjectives use **more** and **most** instead of adding *er* and *est*.
For example: *His tea was delicious. Her tea was **more** delicious, but my tea was the **most** delicious.*

3 Fill the gaps with the correct adjectives.

a A crab can be dangerous, a jellyfish is _____ dangerous but a shark is the _____ dangerous.

b Before the school concert, the parents were _____, the teachers were _____ nervous but the children were the _____ nervous.

c Tim found the movie _____ exciting than Ashley did.

d I think that Mandy Lynne is the _____ talented member of the group.

Some adjectives are completely different when comparing. For example: *good, better, best*

4 Write adjectives to complete the following groups.

a bad, _____ , worst   b little, less, _____

c well, _____ , best

CHALLENGE

On a separate piece of paper, draw your own three-panel comic strip based
on the adjectives that compare one of the following:

weak   sad   wet   fat   tiny   ugly   clever   interesting

Zelda

She wrestles writhing, scaly serpents that hiss and sputter deadly poison.

I'll adjust the idle arm and she'll begin running like a dream.

KLINK   KLINK

She bravely fights and conquers fearsome and frightening dragons that spit fiery breath.

For today only ...special deal...it's a bargain... blah, blah, blah...

Not today, thank you sonny.

She boldly drives off aggressive, angry, invading aliens.

Shoo, spidey.

She uses her magic wand to tame huge, hairy, many-legged monsters waiting to pounce upon her at an unsuspecting moment.

WHIIRRRR

She desperately grapples and struggles with cold-hearted, unfriendly robots who seek to control the Earth.

Is she a tired, old, confused grandmother? NO!
She is ZELDA...
Gritty Granny of Steel,
Noble Nan of Knowledge,
Nimble Nonny of Note,
She is...

ZELDA - SUPERGRAN

OXFORD UNIVERSITY PRESS

We can use articles (a, an, the) and adjectives to make nouns more interesting.
For example: *the little, red car*   *a ripe, juicy pear*   *an elegant ballerina*
These word groups are called noun groups.

1 Use noun groups from the text on page 16 to answer these questions.

a   Who or what sputter deadly poison? _____

b   Who or what seek to control the Earth? _____

c   What do frightening dragons spit? _____

d   Who or what are waiting to pounce on Zelda? _____

_____

e   What does Zelda use to tame monsters? _____

f   Who or what does Zelda boldly drive off? _____

2 Write the three noun groups used to describe Zelda – SUPERGRAN!_____

_____

_____

_____

3 Which article, *a* or *an*, would correctly complete these noun groups?

a   _____ angry alien

b   _____ ordinary, black book

c   _____ beautiful, floral display

d   _____ university education

e   _____ old, brown, cattle dog

f   _____ rickety, old staircase

g   _____ big, red, juicy apple

h   _____ ancient, hidden burial site

CHALLENGE

On a separate piece of paper or on a computer, write or type your own noun groups, each containing an article (*a, an, the*) and an adjective, using these nouns.

a   shark   b   volcano   c   wizard   d   racing car

Medusa the Gorgon
(a Greek myth)

The Gorgons were three beautiful sisters. One of the sisters, Medusa, was famous for her glorious hair, which flowed in golden locks down her back.

Medusa unknowingly offended the goddess Athena by taking shelter and being disrespectful in one of her temples. Athena was outraged. She changed Medusa into a winged monster with glaring eyes, a protruding tongue, scaly skin and razor-sharp claws. Worst of all for the once beautiful maiden, her gorgeous hair became writhing, poisonous serpents. Athena had created such a hideous monster that those who gazed upon her were instantly turned to stone.

The hero Perseus was sent by the king Polydectes to slay the horrible Gorgon. He was helped in his task by the gods Athena, who gave him a brightly polished shield, Hermes, who gave him a sharp sickle, a strong leather bag and a pair of winged sandals, and Hades, who gave him a helmet that made the wearer invisible.

Perseus used the winged sandals to fly to the cave in which the monster dwelt. There he put on the helmet of invisibility and entered Medusa's lair.

Medusa was aware of the hero's presence and the furious creature prepared to attack and kill the intruder by whatever means she could.

Perseus, however, used the shield to avoid staring directly at the Gorgon. By looking at the reflection, he was able to approach and when she had slithered close to him, with one mighty blow of the sickle he lopped off the creature's head. From Medusa's blood sprang the magnificent winged horse Pegasus.

Perseus placed the severed head of Medusa into his leather bag, climbed onto the back of Pegasus and flew back to the palace of King Polydectes to show him the trophy. This marked the beginning of many adventures for the hero, but for the hideous beast that Medusa the Gorgon had become it was a sad and violent end.

OXFORD UNIVERSITY PRESS

1 Use the codes shown below to write whether the following words from the story are:

> common nouns (CN), proper nouns (PN), or adjectives (A)

a Medusa _____

b Athena _____

c glorious _____

d goddess _____

e hideous _____

f protruding _____

g Pegasus _____

h monster _____

i helmet _____

j poisonous _____

k magnificent _____

l Hermes _____

2 Write adjectives used in the story on page 18 to describe the following:

a _____ sisters

b _____ sandals

c _____ claws

d _____ eyes

e _____ tongue

f _____ sickle

g _____ bag

3 Write suitable articles (*a* or *an*) to complete these noun groups.

a _____ invisibility helmet

b _____ offended goddess

c _____ polished shield

d _____ magnificent winged horse

e _____ adventurous hero

f _____ writhing serpent

CHALLENGE

Use the following noun groups to help you write your own adventure about Perseus and his winged horse Pegasus. Finish on a separate piece of paper or on your computer if you need to.

> a cruel monster   a tentacled sea creature   an eerie forest
> an angry goddess   the king's luxurious palace   a slow and dangerous climb

_____

_____

_____

_____

_____

_____

TOPIC 1: ASSESS YOUR GRAMMAR!

Nouns, adjectives and noun groups

1 Shade the bubble next to the common noun.

⚪ sorrow ⚪ pillow ⚪ Mr Pinto ⚪ magical

2 Shade the bubble next to the abstract noun.

⚪ luck ⚪ Holden ⚪ flock ⚪ student

3 Shade the bubble next to the collective noun for **flowers**.

⚪ flock ⚪ herd ⚪ bouquet ⚪ punnet

4 Shade the bubble next to the proper noun.

⚪ march ⚪ China ⚪ person ⚪ clever

5 Shade the bubble next to the abstract noun.

⚪ piston ⚪ engine ⚪ freedom ⚪ tube

6 Shade the bubble next to the word that is an incorrect plural noun.

⚪ radios ⚪ tomatoes ⚪ potatos ⚪ pianos

7 Shade the bubble next to the best adjective to describe **food**.

⚪ shaggy ⚪ fierce ⚪ delicious ⚪ peaceful

8 Shade the word that cannot be used as an adjective.

⚪ sweet ⚪ smart ⚪ once ⚪ quiet

OXFORD UNIVERSITY PRESS

9 Shade the bubble next to the adjective that would complete this group: **bad**, **worse** ...

○ badder   ○ baddest   ○ worst   ○ worsest

10 Shade the bubble next to the noun group.

○ a long, thin plank   ○ running quickly   ○ waiting patiently   ○ Sammi ate dinner.

Use words from the box to complete each definition below.

> a proper noun, an adjective, a common noun, a pronoun, an abstract noun

11 A word that describes a noun is called _____ .

12 A word that names ordinary things, people and places is called _____ .

13 A word that names things that you cannot see or touch, such as feelings, is called

_____ .

14 A word that names special things, people and places is called _____ .

HOW AM I DOING?

Tick the boxes if you understand.

Common nouns name people, things and places. ☐

Abstract nouns name feelings and qualities (you cannot see or touch them). ☐

Collective nouns name groups of people or things. ☐

Proper nouns are special names for people, places and things. ☐

Plural nouns name more than one. ☐

Adjectives describe nouns. ☐

Adjectives can be used to compare characters. ☐

A noun group can consist of an article (**a**, **an** or **the**), adjectives and a noun. ☐

UNIT 2.1 Verbs

The Verbs

It's Sunday in the suburbs and the Verbs begin to stir.

Mick, the Verb dog, howls.
Danny Verb wakes late again.

Vera Verb thinks her breakfast is delicious. Yummy!

Grandaddy Verb mows the lawn.

Granny Verb washes the car.

Herbie Verb waters the geraniums.

Daddy Verb reads the paper.

Mummy Verb rides her skateboard and ...

... little Baby Verb cries because ...

... Collingwood loses the footy again!

OXFORD UNIVERSITY PRESS

Verbs tell us what is happening in a sentence. They tell us what has been done, is being done or will be done. Verbs can be doing, saying, thinking or feeling verbs. All sentences must have at least one verb in them. For example:

*The children **jumped**.* (doing verb) *Mum **called**.* (saying verb) *I **wondered**.* (thinking verb)
*We **like** ...* (feeling verb)

1 Use verbs from the comic strip 'The Verbs' to help you fill in the gaps in these sentences. On the line at the end of the sentence write whether the verb is a doing, saying, thinking or feeling verb.

a   Danny _____ late again.   _____

b   Mick, the Verb dog, _____ .   _____

c   "Yummy!" _____ Vera Verb.   _____

d   Mummy Verb _____ her skateboard.   _____

e   "Wah! We lost the footy again!" _____ Baby Verb.   _____

Verbs can also be being or having words. When on their own, these verbs are called relating verbs.
Relating verbs that are being words: *am, is, are, was, were*
Relating verbs that are having words: *has, have, had*

2 Write four different relating verbs that best fit in these sentences. (More than one verb may be suitable.)

a   I _____ over here.   b   Baby Verb _____ on the mat.

c   Herbie _____ a hose.   d   _____ Mummy Verb nearby?

e   They _____ late.   f   Do you _____ a skateboard?

g   Vera _____ hungry.   h   We _____ at the football.

When being or having verbs are used with another verb, we call them helping or auxiliary verbs.
For example: *The Verbs are waking.*
The doing verb in this sentence is *waking*, and *are* is the auxiliary verb.

3 Write suitable auxiliary verbs to help the underlined verbs in these sentences.

a   Daddy Verb _____ <u>pondering</u> the news in the paper.

b   Grandaddy _____ <u>started mowing</u> the lawn.

c   Granny _____ outside <u>washing</u> the car.

d   Herbie Verb _____ <u>watering</u> the geraniums.

CHALLENGE

On a separate piece of paper or on a computer, write or type a list of six things that you might do on the weekend. If possible, include a doing, saying, thinking and feeling verb.

A song of wind

Hark to the song of the scattering, scurrying
Blustering, bullying, bellowing, hurrying wind!
Over the hills it comes, laughing and rollicking,
Curling and whirling, flying and frolicking,
Spinning the clouds that are scattered and thinned,
And shouting a song
As it gallops along —
A song that is nothing but wind.

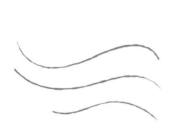

This is the song of the galloping, hurrying,
Gusty, and dusty, and whirling, and worrying wind.
Over the hill it comes laughing and rollicking,
Yelling, and swooping, and flying, and frolicking,
Shaking the fences so solidly pinned,
And shrieking a song
As it gallops along —
A terrible song that is wind.

Will Lawson

OXFORD UNIVERSITY PRESS

Verbs tell us what is being done, said, thought or felt in a sentence. Writers choose verbs to give precise meaning so the audience can visualise what they mean. For example: *shouting, whispering, shrieking*
Verbs can also be having (*had, has, have*) or being (*am, are, is, was, were*) words.
Verbs that have only one word are called simple verbs. For example: *The wind **hurried** over the hill.*
Some verbs have two parts. These are called compound verbs or verb groups.

1 Read the poem. Find verbs to complete the sentences below telling what the wind is doing.

a   The wind is _____.   b   The wind is _____.

c   The wind is _____.   d   The wind is _____.

> Compound verbs are made up of a helping verb (*auxiliary verb*) and a *main verb*. For example: *have walked, is playing, will catch*

2 Write whether the verbs below are simple verbs or compound verbs.

a   comes _____   b   is laughing _____

c   is rollicking _____   d   curls _____

e   is swooping _____   f   gallops _____

Verbs take different forms to show the time something happened, is happening or will happen.
We call this verb tense. It tells us whether the action happened in the past, is happening in the present or will happen in the future. For example: *I walked.* (past) *I am walking.* (present)
I will walk. (future) Note: *am* and *will* are auxiliary (helping) verbs.

3 Write whether the underlined words are past, present or future tense verbs.

a   The wind **is shrieking**. _____

b   The clouds **were spinning**. _____

c   He **sold** all of his basketball cards. _____

d   The farmer **will plough** his field in spring. _____

e   Tessa **is skating** very well. _____

f   Indy **slid** down the vine to the forest floor below. _____

g   The ship **will sail** through the heads at dusk. _____

h   The children **are waiting** in a line outside. _____

4 Write the auxiliary (helping) verbs used in Question 3 above.

_____   _____   _____   _____

CHALLENGE

a   Read the poem again and circle the five saying verbs used.

b   Circle the doing verb below you might use when the wind is moving the fastest.

> rollicking   frolicking   swooping   flying   galloping

c   Write a verb from the poem that has the same meaning as *listen*. _____

d   On a separate piece of paper or on a computer, write a list of doing verbs that tell some of the things done by your five senses. For example: *sniff, lick, look*

Atom Andy

Atom Andy is waking.

BRRR

Atom Andy has woken, showered, eaten and dressed ready for another day at the Super Deeds office.

Atom Andy is leaving home.

Atom Andy has walked, hopped, skipped, run, swum, flown and crawled his way to work.

Atom Andy is receiving his first emergency call for the day.

Atom, come quickly!

Atom Andy has raced, hurried and sped to the scene of the emergency.

Mrs Atom Andy has given Atom his cut lunch, which he had left on the kitchen bench.

OXFORD UNIVERSITY PRESS

Verbs not only tell us what is happening in a sentence, they also tell us when the action takes place. This is called verb tense. Verb tense tells us whether the action happened in the past, is happening in the present or will happen in the future.

For example: **slept** (past), **is sleeping** (present), **will sleep** (future)

Helping or auxiliary verbs help to tell us the tense of a sentence.

For example: **was flowing** (**was**, the auxiliary, tells us the tense is past)

is flowing (**is**, the auxiliary, tells us the tense is present)

will flow (**will**, the auxiliary, tells us the tense is future)

1 Identify and write the auxiliary verb and verb tense (write *past*, *present* or *future*) of these sentences.

a Atom Andy has woken. **auxiliary verb** _____ tense _____

b Our hero will hurry to the scene. _____ tense _____

c Andy is receiving his first emergency call. _____ tense _____

d Mrs Andy has given Atom Andy his lunch. _____ tense _____

e Andy's wife and his dog are waiting for him. _____ tense _____

f The Super Flakes were sitting on the kitchen table. _____ tense _____

2 Rewrite these sentences as past tense by changing the auxiliary verb.

For example: *I **am** walking. I **was** walking.*

a They are eating their lunches. _____

b I am writing a story about a strange fish. _____

_____

c Mai will bite her apple. _____

_____

CHALLENGE

Write the following verbs in the past, present and future tense using auxiliary verbs when necessary.

a steal _____ _____ _____

b break _____ _____ _____

c see _____ _____ _____

d catch _____ _____ _____

e buy _____ _____ _____

A day in the life of a superhero

Adverb Man is an extremely busy superhero. Here, for the first time, we can get a glimpse of a superhero's typical day by looking at a few pages in the diary of Adverb Man.

Monday 6 a.m. – 6:01 a.m.

I jumped quickly into the nearest telephone box and changed into my Adverb Man costume.

11 a.m.

I desperately raced along the freeway to overtake and stop a runaway fuel tanker, which was charging headlong towards a group of school children.

7:31 p.m.

I was arrested and charged with several crimes.

7 a.m.

I flew swiftly into space to collide with a stray comet that was hurtling furiously towards Earth.

2:30 p.m.

I powerfully burst my way through the wall of the State Bank to arrest the Beedle Boys, who were attempting to blow the safe.

POW!

9 a.m.

I used my secret heat vision to glare intensely at an iceberg, which was threatening to sink the extremely famous ocean liner Icy Titan.

ICY TITAN

5 – 7:30 p.m.

With the Saturn volcano threatening to abruptly explode and bury the east coast in ash and lava, I burrowed quickly to the centre of the Earth and plugged the lava flow, thereby saving millions of lives.

Police Arrest Sheet

Name: A. Man

Age: unknown

Address: T. Box

1 Undressing in a public place (and littering).
2 Endangering low-flying aircraft and flying without a pilot's licence.
3 Carrying a concealed weapon (which Mr Man referred to as his 'heat vision').
4 Speeding. Mr Man clocked 110 km/h in an 80 km/h zone.
5 Vandalism, in that Mr Man destroyed the wall of the State Bank.
6 Environmental damage and mining without a licence.

Comments by arresting officer PC Koreckt: We threw the book at Mr Man but it just bounced off him.

NEWS FLASH!

Mr Man was arrested after several complaints from the public. He has been charged with the following...

OXFORD UNIVERSITY PRESS

Adverbs add to the meaning of verbs (*jumped* **quickly**) or sometimes adjectives (**extremely** *loud*).
Adverbs tell how, when, where or how often.
For example: *Adverb Man jumped quickly into the telephone box.* How did he jump? **quickly**

He will be arrested later. When will he be arrested? **later**

A-Man threw his clothes outside. Where did he throw them? **outside**

He does heroic things every day. How often does he do them? **every day**

1 Find adverbs from the story that tell *how* about these verbs. For example: *jumped – quickly*

a flew _____   b raced _____   c burst _____

d explode _____   e hurtling _____   f burrowed _____

g glare _____   h charging _____

2 Write whether the underlined adverbs tell *how, when, where* or *how often* about the verb.

a Adverb Man gets into trouble with the police regularly. _____

b PC Koreckt dutifully arrested the culprit. _____

c The comet crashed violently into Adverb Man's tightly clenched fist. _____

d He landed here. _____

e The bank on Main Street has already been robbed twice. _____

f Adverb Man had a very busy day yesterday. _____

g The lava gushed ferociously _____ and began to spread everywhere. _____

h Patiently the Beedle Boys waited until the safe exploded noisily. _____

3 Find adverbs in the story that have been formed from these adjectives.

a desperate _____   b intense _____   c extreme _____

d powerful _____   e quick _____   f abrupt _____

g furious _____   h swift _____

4 Replace the underlined groups of words with suitable adverbs.

a The passengers gazed at the melting iceberg with hope. _____

b The volcano erupted with a loud noise. _____

c He lifted the boulder with ease. _____

d She had only seen the show one time. _____

CHALLENGE

On a separate piece of paper or on a computer, write or type four sentences about a superhero. Your first sentence should include an adverb of place (**where**), your second an adverb of time (**when**), your third an adverb of manner (**how**) and your final sentence should include an adverb of degree (**how often**).

The adventures of Willy Maykit

OXFORD UNIVERSITY PRESS

Some verbs are used with the main verb to give us an idea of the degree to which something might happen. They tell us the level of certainty or probability of something happening.

The text on page 30 shows three levels of certainty:

*Willy **might** jump.* (Willy is thinking about jumping, so this is low certainty.)

*Willy **should** jump.* (Willy hears a rumbling, so his thoughts about jumping have increased to a medium level of certainty.)

*Willy **must** jump.* (Willy needs to jump to escape the rampaging razorbacks, so jumping has become a certainty.)

The verbs *might*, *should* and *must* are called modal verbs.

1 Underline the modal verbs in these sentences.

   a   I might go to the cinema tonight.

   b   The boys will build their shelter on the beach.

   c   "You need to write in your exercise books," said Ms Lewis.

   d   When she sees that mess she could be angry.

   e   "You may leave when the bell rings," said Mr Rosso.

   f   Perhaps you should wear your raincoat today.

Modal verbs are auxiliary (helping) verbs.

Some adverbs can be modal adverbs. Modal adverbs can be used with verbs to add a degree of certainty or possibility. For example: ***Perhaps** you dropped your wallet. It seems **likely**.*
*He **definitely** needs a new wallet.*
Perhaps, *likely* and *definitely* are modal adverbs, because they tell us more about what is possible or certain.

2 Choose a modal adverb from the box to vary the degree of certainty in these sentences.

> certainly   never   probably   absolutely   always

   a   The boy had trouble passing his exams because he _____ studied.

   b   "I am _____ sure I am a prince," said Rupert.

   c   It is _____ cold in winter.

   d   Willy would _____ have been scared when he heard the stampeding animals behind him.

   e   Willy _____ panicked when the razorbacks appeared.

CHALLENGE

On a separate piece of paper or on a computer, write or type sentences of your own containing these modal verbs and adverbs.

> might   must   possibly   definitely

Preppo Boy at the pool

Preppo Boy is spending his day off at the local pool. He arrives very early in the morning and finds a great spot near the kiosk.

Preppo Boy climbs up the ladder of the Giant Waterslide.

At the top, he decides not to slide today.

Preppo tries to bomb some girls from his school. Perhaps his bomb might have been better if the girls hadn't been sunbathing on the concrete path.

Preppo is on the high diving board. He does a triple somersault followed by a backflip, half twist and pike. His entry into the water is perfect. When Preppo surfaces, he remembers that he hasn't learnt to swim yet.

Later, Preppo hogs the wading pool with his bathtub toys.

Preppo flicks somebody's bottom with his wet towel. I wonder if the lifeguard was ready for a dip?

Before lunchtime, Preppo Boy is flying through the gate of the pool. The lifeguard thinks that Preppo Boy should go back to his job protecting the weak and defenceless from the forces of evil and naughtiness.

OXFORD UNIVERSITY PRESS

Prepositional phrases add details to a sentence, often telling how, when, where or why something happened. Prepositional phrases begin with a preposition.

For example: *Nikki took the book **from her bag**.*   prepositional phrase telling **where**

                 *She opened the book and started to read **in a soft voice**.*   prepositional phrase telling **how**

Some common prepositions are:

about	along	before	between	from	on (onto)	through	until
above	among	behind	by	in	out (out of)	to	up
across	around	below	during	into	over	towards	with
after	at	beside	for	near	past	under	without

1 Read 'Preppo Boy at the pool', then write prepositions from the list above that are also in the comic strip. _____

2 Rewrite these sentences with the opposite meaning by changing the prepositions.

   a The helicopter flew over the power lines. _____

       _____

   b We will hear the school band play before lunch. _____

       _____

   c A frog hopped off the lily pad. _____

       _____

3 Make up your own prepositional phrases that begin with these prepositions, and then write each prepositional phrase in a sentence.

   For example: **beside**   *We sat beside the pool.*

   a across _____

   b below _____

   c over _____

4 Rewrite these sentences, without changing the meaning, so that they begin with a prepositional phrase.

   a Preppo Boy is hogging the wading pool with his bathtub toys. _____

       _____

   b He was flying out of the gate before lunchtime. _____

       _____

CHALLENGE

On a separate piece of paper or on a computer, make up your own sentence containing a prepositional phrase. Next, write your sentence in as many different ways as you can by only changing the preposition.

For example: *I jumped **over** the creek. I jumped **into** the creek.*

Bernhard, *otherwise known as Barney*, gets ready for school

Mum gets Bernhard ready for school ...

"Scrub your hands, brush your teeth and neatly comb your hair;

Now let me rub some sunscreen on your skin so fair.

Fine clean underwear and a singlet for the cold,

A hanky for your pocket — I'll give it one more fold.

Shined-up black shoes and socks pulled high,

A smartly ironed cotton shirt — do you need a tie?

My, those creases in your blue jeans do look neat.

Um! A woolly cap or sunhat to shield you from the heat?

I've packed you up a healthy lunch of nuts and fruit,

I wonder if I should have made you wear your suit?

Have you got the 'holli snaps' for tell and show?

My, don't you look a treat — so off you go."

Bernhard, otherwise known as Barney, gets himself ready for school ...

Marbles in my alley bag, trade cards in my pocket,

Spidey in my treasure box (I'd better not unlock it).

Yoyo on my finger and fake tatt on my hand,

(Would have got a real one but at school they're banned).

Footy underneath my arm and skateboard under feet,

Cicada on my stained shirt that says 'GO HEAT'.

Got my new power game that's called 'Killer Hawk',

And my slurpy, slimy, sludge Sloppa for morning talk.

"How about some loose change, Mum, for me to buy my lunch?

I'll just get a pie with sauce and chips to munch."

I'll wear my shorts backwards cos that's really cool.

Whoa! It's nearly 10 past 9. I'd better get to school!

OXFORD UNIVERSITY PRESS

A phrase is a group of words without a verb or action word. A phrase that starts with a preposition is called a prepositional phrase.

For example: *in the park, at school, with a red nose*

Some prepositional phrases add details about a noun or pronoun.

For example: The man **with long hair** plays in a rock band.

The phrase *with long hair* tells us more about the man.

1 Read the poems on page 34 and then underline the prepositional phrases in each sentence below. (Each phrase begins with a preposition.)

a   The marbles in this alley bag are mine.   b   The footy underneath my arm is old.

c   The cicada on my stained shirt is cool.   d   I am eating a pie with sauce.

e   The skateboard under his feet is cracked.   f   The yoyo on my finger is yellow.

Some prepositional phrases add details about the action in a sentence. They tell us how, when, where and why the action in the sentence is performed. For example:

i   *The children clapped **with enthusiasm**.*
    The phrase *with enthusiasm* tells us how the children clapped.

ii   **By this afternoon** *the rain will clear.*
    The phrase *by this afternoon* tells us when the rain will clear.

iii   *Let me rub sunscreen **on your skin**.*
    The phrase *on your skin* tells us where the sunscreen is rubbed.

iv   **Because of the bad weather** *the sports were cancelled.*
    The phrase *because of the bad weather* tells us why the sports were cancelled.

2 Underline the prepositional phrases in each sentence and write whether they are telling how, when, where or why. For example: *They are banned* <u>at school</u>.   (where)

a   Barney drew a tattoo on his hand. _____

b   He arrived after the bell had rung. _____

c   Bernhard wore a singlet for the cold. _____

d   The creases were in his blue jeans. _____

e   During the morning, he gave a talk on his sludge Sloppa. _____

f   Mr Craig answered in an angry voice. _____

g   "I'm late, I'd better run to school," said Barney. _____

CHALLENGE

On a separate piece of paper or on a computer, write or type sentences of your own that begin with these prepositional phrases.

a   After midnight ...   b   Under the bridge ...   c   In the centre of the circle ...

d   Across the sky ...   e   With a huge sigh ...   f   On his head ...

Gulnara

This is a Russian story of Gulnara, the Tartar warrior.

Gulnara was strong and brave and she had magical powers. One day, seeking adventure, Gulnara rode from her village to join an army that was fighting the evil wizard and warlord Khan Kuzlan. After riding for two days, Gulnara reached the encampment of the army. The men of that army laughed heartily when Gulnara said she wanted to join them.

They said, "You are just a girl. We don't want to fight with a girl. War is for men. Go back to your village you silly girl."

Gulnara ignored the men and went to see the chief of the army. He was a wise leader and knew that there was something special about this girl. Despite the protests of his soldiers he invited Gulnara to ride with his army.

Soon the army arrived at a wide, rapidly flowing river. There was no way across, but the tents of Kuzlan's army could be clearly seen on the other side of the river.

That night, while the men of both armies slept soundly, Gulnara magically transformed into a hawk. In this guise, she flew across the river to spy upon Kuzlan and his army. She then soared back into the sky and glided up and down the river until her sharp eyes caught sight of a hidden footbridge spanning the water.

Back at camp and once more in her human form, Gulnara told the chief of her discovery. The chief immediately ordered Gulnara to lead a group of soldiers across the footbridge and into Kuzlan's camp. Gulnara and the soldiers stealthily crept into the enemy camp only to find it seemingly deserted — there was no sign of the evil Kuzlan or his army anywhere.

"You see," said the soldiers, "a girl cannot lead men. Let us return to our camp and tell the chief that we have defeated Kuzlan and his army has run off back to their villages." The soldiers then returned to their camp.

Gulnara, however, continued to search the encampment. She soon came across a camel with two bags of sand straddled across its back. Gulnara tied a rope around the beast's neck and led it back to her camp.

Upon seeing Gulnara approach, the chief called to her, "Gulnara, my soldiers have returned with the good news that our enemy is defeated!"

Gulnara could not help but laugh.

"See for yourself, my Lord," she said while smacking the camel forcefully upon its rump. Before the eyes of everyone the camel changed its form and became the wizard Khan Kuzlan. The bags fell to the ground spilling the sand and each grain became a soldier so that shortly Kuzlan's entire army stood helplessly within the enemy camp.

Immediately Kuzlan and his whole army were imprisoned. Gulnara had gained the respect of her fellow soldiers and the chief appointed her second-in-command of his army.

OXFORD UNIVERSITY PRESS

1 Underline or circle the verbs in these sentences from the story of Gulnara.

a The men of that army laughed heartily at Gulnara.

b After riding for two days, Gulnara reached the encampment of the army.

c Gulnara and the soldiers stealthily crept into the enemy camp.

d Immediately Kuzlan and his whole army were imprisoned.

e They said, "You are just a girl."

f Soon the army arrived at a wide, rapidly flowing river.

2 Write adverbs from the story that best tell more about these verbs.

a _____ crept

b laughed _____

c _____ flowing

d _____ transformed

e _____ imprisoned

f _____ arrived (when)

g stood _____

h _____ deserted

3 Write the prepositions that could complete these phrases from the story.

a _____ the enemy camp

b _____ the river

c _____ her village

d _____ the footbridge

CHALLENGE

Write sentences of your own containing these adverbs from the story of Gulnara.

a shortly _____

_____

b forcefully _____

_____

c magically _____

_____

TOPIC 2: ASSESS YOUR GRAMMAR!

Verbs, adverbs and prepositional phrases

1 Shade the bubble next to the type of **verb** underlined in this sentence.

Dad asked us if we wanted to come to the game with him.

○ doing verb　　　○ saying verb　　　○ thinking verb　　　○ feeling verb

2 Shade the bubble next to the type of **verb** underlined in this sentence.

The soldiers marched from the camp to the top of the hill.

○ doing verb　　　○ saying verb　　　○ thinking verb　　　○ feeling verb

3 Shade the bubble next to the type of **verb** underlined in this sentence.

"I wish I had a camera," laughed Paul.

○ doing verb　　　○ saying verb　　　○ thinking verb　　　○ feeling verb

4 Shade the bubble next to the type of **verb** underlined in this sentence.

"Imagine you are on a yacht sailing on the Pacific Ocean," said Catelin.

○ doing verb　　　○ saying verb　　　○ thinking verb　　　○ feeling verb

5 Shade the bubble beneath the **relating verb** in this sentence.

The players were on the bus.

　　　○　　○　○　　○

6 Write a suitable **auxiliary verb** to make this sentence past tense.

The leaves [_____] *rustling in the treetops.*

7 Write a suitable **auxiliary verb** to make this sentence present tense.

The children [_____] *waiting at the entrance to the zoo.*

OXFORD UNIVERSITY PRESS

8 Write a suitable auxiliary verb to make this sentence future tense.

We [   ] catch colds if we don't wear our coats.

9 Shade the bubble beneath the adverb in this sentence.

Sammi and Karl waited quietly in the main corridor.

○   ○   ○   ○

10 Shade the bubble beneath the modal verb in this sentence.

"If we hurry, kids, we could be the first to arrive," called Henry, our group leader.

○   ○   ○   ○

11 Write a suitable modal adverb to complete this sentence.

By the size of their win, the Comets will [   ] finish on top of the ladder.

12 Complete the following sentence using a prepositional phrase telling **where**.

The homeless man slept [   ].

13 Complete the following sentence using a prepositional phrase telling **when**.

[   ] I went to the movies with my friends.

HOW AM I DOING?

Tick the boxes if you understand.

Verbs can be doing, saying, thinking or feeling verbs. ☐

Verbs can tell us when action takes place. This is called **tense**. ☐

Adverbs add to the meaning of verbs. ☐

A prepositional phrase begins with a preposition and adds details to a sentence. ☐

Might, should and *must* are modal verbs. They tell us the likelihood of something happening. ☐

So you want to be a clown!

So you want to be a clown! Here are some tips for you on the best way to achieve your goal.

You will need ... a bucketful of foolishness, a sackful of silliness, a spoonful of sadness and ... a dash of happiness is helpful!

Be graceful when arriving, graceless when entering and hopeless when leaving.

For transport
... a little tricycle is good
... an odd bicycle is better but
... a monocycle is best!

Tuneful is handy but tuneless is funny.

Silly movements and noisiness could be useful. TWOOP!

A nose that disconnects and a bow tie that moves in an anticlockwise direction will cause amusement.

Nervousness followed by bad judgement will bring a laugh but ... it may bring astronomical doctor's bills, too!

OXFORD UNIVERSITY PRESS

A prefix is a word part that, when added to the beginning of another word or word part, changes the meaning of the word.

For example: By adding *dis-*, *mis-* or *un-* to words, we form antonyms (opposites):
                  disappear, **mis**behave, **un**necessary

1 Add prefixes to the following words to form antonyms (opposites).

a   connect _____   b   clockwise _____

c   understand _____   d   sure _____

2 Some prefixes are used to express a number. For example: *mono* = 1, *bi* = 2, *tri* = 3
Use a dictionary to help you complete the following.

a   Write three words that begin with the prefix *mono-*.

_____   _____   _____

b   Write three words that begin with the prefix *bi-*.

_____   _____   _____

c   Write three words that begin with the prefix *tri-*.

_____   _____   _____

Suffixes are word endings. Adding a suffix can change the grammatical form of the word (for example, an adjective will become a noun). Some suffixes can also change a word to an antonym (opposite).

3 Change these adjectives to nouns by adding the suffix *-ness*. Remember to change the *y* to *i* first.

a   silly _____   b   noisy _____

c   happy _____   d   empty _____

4 Change these verbs to nouns by adding the suffix *-ment*.

a   amuse _____   b   judge _____

c   move _____   d   agree _____

5 Change these nouns to adjectives by adding the suffix *-ful*.

a   grace _____   b   help _____

c   tune _____   d   use _____

6 Change the suffixes of these words to make them antonyms (opposites).

a   graceful _____   b   careful _____

c   tuneful _____   d   fearful _____

CHALLENGE

How many words can you find and write (on a separate piece of paper or a computer) that begin with the prefixes **trans-** and **astro-**? Use a dictionary to help you.

Tide talk

The tide and I had stopped to chat
About the waves where seabirds sat,
About the yachts with bobbing sails
And quite enormous, spouting whales.

The tide has lots to talk about.
Sometimes it's in. Sometimes it's out.
For something you must understand,
It's up and down across the sand;
Sometimes it's low and sometimes it's high.
It's very wet and never dry.

The tide, quite crossly, said: "The sea
Is always out there pushing me.
And just when I am feeling slack,
It sends me in then drags me back.
It never seems to let me go.
I rise. I fall. I'm to and fro."

I told the tide, "I know it's true
For I am pushed around like you.
And really do they think it's fair?
Do this. Do that. Come here. Go there."
Then loudly came my parents' shout.
So I went in.
The tide went out.

Max Fatchen

OXFORD UNIVERSITY PRESS

Antonyms are words that have opposite meanings. Writers often use antonyms to compare and contrast as they build a description or set a scene.

For example: *big* and *small* are antonyms; *light* and *dark* are antonyms.

1 Match words in the poem that are antonyms for these.

a   up _____

b   in _____

c   wet _____

d   low _____

e   pulling _____

f   rise _____

g   fro _____

h   come _____

i   tiny _____

j   tight _____

k   this _____

l   started _____

m   quietly _____

n   always _____

o   stood _____

Some antonyms can be formed by adding prefixes (beginnings).

For example: *common/uncommon*   *approve/disapprove*

2 Add the prefixes *un-* or *dis-* to change these words to antonyms.

a   _____true

b   _____fair

c   _____appear

d   _____do

e   _____like

f   _____trust

g   _____likely

h   _____popular

i   _____obey

j   _____happy

k   _____safe

l   _____known

m   _____honest

n   _____pleasant

o   ____advantage

p   _____loyal

q   _____approval

r   _____able

s   _____lock

t   _____selfish

3 Add the prefixes *im-* or *in-* to change these words to antonyms.

a   _____possible

b   _____accurate

c   _____visible

d   _____correct

e   _____patient

f   _____mortal

g   _____famous

h   _____polite

i   _____direct

j   _____proper

k   _____mature

l   _____sane

Some antonyms can be formed by changing the suffixes (endings). For example: *careful/careless*

4 Write antonyms by changing the suffix.

a   useful _____

b   merciful _____

c   cheerful _____

d   hopeless _____

e   pitiless _____

f   joyful _____

CHALLENGE

Change these words to antonyms (opposites) by changing the prefix.

a   increase _____

b   outside _____

c   encouraged _____

d   export _____

e   deflate _____

f   interior _____

Recognise that rhyme?

1 Sparkle, sparkle tiny nova
How I question what you are!
Up above the Earth so lofty
Resembling a jewel in the
    atmosphere.

2 A trio of small cats
They misplaced their gloves
And they started to weep.
Oh, mummy dear, we unhappily dread
Our mitts we have mislaid.
The three tiny pussies
They regained their mitts
And they commenced to sob
Oh, mamma dear, see here, see here
Our gloves we have recovered.

3 Aged Mama Hubbard
Went to the pantry
To get her miserable
    hound a fossil
But when she got there
The larder was empty
And so the wretched
    bow-wow had zilch.

4 Hey, diddle, diddle, the puss and the violin
The heifer leapt over the moon
The wee puppy chortled to witness such amusement
While the bowl dashed away with the ladle.

5 Jack be agile,
Jack be swift,
Jack vault over
    the lantern.

6 Jack and Jill
Travelled up the slope
To obtain a bucket of H_2O
Jack tumbled down
And fractured his head
And Jill came toppling later.

OXFORD UNIVERSITY PRESS

A synonym is a word with a similar meaning to another word.

For example: **great**: massive, huge, big, vast, enormous, large

spin: twist, turn, revolve, whirl, twirl

The nursery rhymes on the opposite page are not in their original form. The original words are written below. Write the synonyms from each rhyme.

1 diamond _____   high _____   like _____

little _____   sky _____   star _____

twinkle _____   wonder _____   world _____

2 began _____   cry _____   fear _____

found _____   kittens _____   little _____

lost _____   mittens _____   Mother _____

sadly _____   three _____

3 bare _____   bone _____   cupboard _____

dog _____   fetch _____   Mother _____

none _____   old _____   poor _____

4 cat _____   cow _____   dish _____

dog _____   fiddle _____   fun _____

jumped _____   laughed _____   little _____

ran _____   see _____   spoon _____

5 candlestick _____   jump _____   nimble _____

quick _____

6 after _____   broke _____   crown _____

fell _____   fetch _____   hill _____

pail _____   tumbling _____   water _____

went _____

CHALLENGE

On a separate piece of paper or on a computer, write or type a short story that includes synonyms for these words.

big brave cry talk small long wet fast nice good

Erik the Viking

Erik was a Viking, brave and bold,
Erik lived in Denmark in days of old.
Erik wore two horns upon his head
And "Toot! Toot! Toot!" those hornies said.
Now Erik set sail on his monthly raid
Looking for a country to invade.
The people of England with hearts drum-drumming
All cried out, "Erik's a-coming!"

When Erik set foot on that northern coast
He searched everywhere for his Anglo host,
But they'd all vanished a-scoot-scoot-scootin'
Far, far away from Erik's toot-tootin'.

With no Saxon peasants to pillage and rob,
Erik started looking for another job.
He checked all the job boards throughout the land
And then formed a Danish rock'n'roll band.

So now when you visit your music shop
To buy some tunes that go hip-hop,
There behind the Songs of Sig and Sven
Will be *Erik's Greatest Hits — Volume 10.*

OXFORD UNIVERSITY PRESS

Pronouns can take the place of nouns. We use them so that we do not have to constantly repeat nouns.

For example: Instead of *Erik was a Viking. Erik was brave and Erik was bold.*

          ... we can write: *Erik was a Viking.* **He** *was brave and* **he** *was bold.*

The main pronouns are *I, you, he, she, it, we, you, they, me, him, her, us* and *them.*

1 Read 'Erik the Viking', then rewrite these sentences using pronouns where appropriate.

a   Erik lived in Denmark and Erik was a Viking. _____

_____

b   The people of England were frightened of Erik because the people of England knew Erik was coming.

_____

_____

c   *Erik's Greatest Hits – Volume 10* is great because *Erik's Greatest Hits – Volume 10* has many fantastic songs on *Erik's Greatest Hits – Volume 10.*

_____

_____

d   Erik could no longer rob the Saxon peasants because Erik had scared the Saxon peasants away.

_____

_____

2 Write the two nouns that have been replaced by the underlined pronouns.

a   Dad was carrying the television into the lounge room when <u>he</u> dropped <u>it</u>.

he: _____   it: _____

b   Andy and I visited Marnie because <u>we</u> had heard <u>she</u> was ill.

we: _____

she: _____

CHALLENGE

Write three sentences about yourself. Include the pronouns **I**, **me** and **you**.

_____

_____

_____

Spruce Sprocket

Ace Detective

★

Our hero, Detective Spruce Sprocket, has stumbled upon the den of the notorious Ned Kelpie and his desperate gang of criminals.

Spruce approaches cautiously and listens while the desperadoes argue about the loot from their latest bank job.

Ha! Ha! All this loot belongs to me. It is mine! mine! mine! I stole it so it's mine! Ha! Ha! Ha!

We helped you steal the loot. That loot is ours. It belongs to us as well.

No it's not. It's mine — you thief, Ned!

They think the loot is theirs — that it belongs to them. Ned thinks that it is his. Nell thinks that it is hers. The Beedle Boys think that the loot is theirs. I have news for all of them. That loot belongs in a bank and they belong behind bars.

OXFORD UNIVERSITY PRESS

Pronouns stand in the place of nouns. Some pronouns are possessive pronouns showing belonging.
Here are the main personal pronouns. (The possessive pronouns are **underlined**.)

First person (about me, about us)   *I, me, mine, we, us, ours (myself, ourselves)*
Second person (about you)   *you, yours (yourself, yourselves)*
Third person (about him, her, them)   *he, she, him, her, his, hers, it, its, they, them, theirs (himself, herself, itself, themselves)*

1   Rewrite these sentences by replacing the repeated (underlined) nouns with pronouns.

a   The loot was stolen by Ned. Ned stole the loot. _____

_____

b   Ned thinks the loot belongs to Ned but Nell thinks the loot belongs to Nell. _____

_____

c   The criminals think that the loot is the criminals'. _____

_____

d   Detective Spruce Sprocket arrived on the scene and Detective Spruce Sprocket arrested

the criminals. _____

_____

2   Use the possessive pronouns shown in the explanation box above to fill the gaps.

a   I stole the loot so it's _____.

b   The criminals thought that the loot was _____ to keep.

c   Nell thinks that the loot should be _____.

d   Ned thinks that the loot should be _____.

e   The Beedle Boys said, "That loot belongs to us, it is _____."

Who, **whom**, **whose**, **which** and **that** are also pronouns.
We call them relative pronouns. Relative pronouns do two jobs at the same time.
They stand in the place of nouns and they join two sentences.
For example: *The criminal who stole the loot was caught by Sprocket.*
Who refers to the criminal and it also joins these two sentences:
The criminal stole the loot.   The criminal was caught by Sprocket.

> We use pronouns so that we don't have to repeat nouns.
> For example: "Ned stole the loot so the loot is Ned's," said Ned would sound much better as: "I stole the loot so it is mine," said Ned.

3   Circle the relative pronouns in these sentences.

a   My house, which is white, is across the street from my school.

b   The boy who rescued the baby has gone home.

c   The egg that is on the bench can be used in the omelette.

CHALLENGE

On a separate piece of paper or a computer, join the following pairs of sentences by selecting from the relative pronouns **who**, **whom**, **whose** and **which**.

a   I have handed in my homework. I did it last night.

b   At the performance there was a clown. The clown juggled six chainsaws.

c   We heard the crack of the gun. The crack signalled the start of the race.

Aunty Em's A.N.T.T.I. E.M. Machine

In a quiet suburban street, Aunty Em looks secretively over her shoulder then climbs into the back of a semi-trailer. Once inside, she sits before her Anti-Nuclear Time Transfer Interface on her Export Machine (A.N.T.T.I. E.M. for short) and fastens her safety harness before flicking some switches.

Flick! "Transporter – ON!"

Flick! "Translator – ON!"

Flick! "Transmitter – ON!"

Flick! "Anti-Matter Pre-Modulator – ON!"

Flick! "Kettle for a nice cup of tea – ON!"

Aunty Em reaches for the Time Transfer dial and turns it slowly until the indicator arrow points to Prehistory. Now Aunty Em is ready. She presses a red button and, at once, she becomes ANTICLOCKWISE WOMAN!

The entire semi-trailer disappears as Anticlockwise Woman begins another fantastic journey.

The A.N.T.T.I. E.M. picks up speed. Faster and faster and faster it whirrs. As a consequence, days turn to months, months to years, years to decades, decades to centuries and centuries to millennia.

Eventually, the A.N.T.T.I. E.M. appears in the steamy, prehistoric jungle of long ago. In due course, Anticlockwise Woman emerges from the machine and briefly scans the scene, until she spots what she has come here for. She quickly gathers a dozen Triceratops eggs before hastily returning to the A.N.T.T.I. E.M.

LATER …

Back in her own time, Aunty Em wins, yet again, for the tenth year in a row, first prize at the local fair's Best Sponge Cake Competition.

People are astounded by her success year after year. In fact, they would give anything to know the secret of Aunty Em's baking success. They just don't know how she does it! However, they do suspect she may be using a secret ingredient!

OXFORD UNIVERSITY PRESS

Signpost words and phrases tell the reader how the text is developing. Signpost words and phrases are called text connectives because they form links between paragraphs, sentences and longer pieces of text.

For example: *It is likely to rain today.* **Therefore** *it might be an idea to take an umbrella.*

Therefore is a text connective because it links two sentences together.

- Text connectives can **clarify**: *in other words, for example, for instance, in fact*
- They can **show cause or result**: *therefore, consequently, as a result, for that reason*
- They can **indicate time or sequence**: *then, next, soon, finally, first, to start with, in conclusion*
- They can **add information**: *in addition, as well, too, what's more, furthermore*
- They can **express a condition or an acknowledgement**: *in that case, however, anyway, yet, on the other hand*

1 Use the text on page 50 to help you write the missing text connectives in these sentences.

a She presses a red button and, _____,

she becomes ANTICLOCKWISE WOMAN!

b _____,

the A.N.T.T.I. E.M. appears in a steamy, prehistoric jungle.

c _____,

days turn to months, months to years and years to decades.

d Back in her own time, Aunty Em wins, _____,

for the tenth year in a row.

e _____, they would give anything to know her secret.

2 Circle the text connectives in this list that indicate time or sequence.

at first	likewise	to begin with	on the other hand
however	in this way	furthermore	at once
next	meanwhile	now	in conclusion

CHALLENGE

On a separate piece of paper or on a computer, use the lists of text connectives at the top of this page to write on one of these topics.

- If I could fly, I would …
- How to make a super smoothie
- Why skateboards should/shouldn't be allowed on footpaths

It's all about the cosmos!

A The giant of our solar system is Jupiter. The planet gets its name from the chief Roman god, known in Greek mythology as Zeus. Jupiter is so large that more than 1000 Earths would fit inside it. It is an incredibly stormy planet too, with a hurricane the size of Earth that has been raging for about 300 years. Of course, you would have trouble surviving on Jupiter, not the least because it is a giant ball of gas — there is no solid surface.

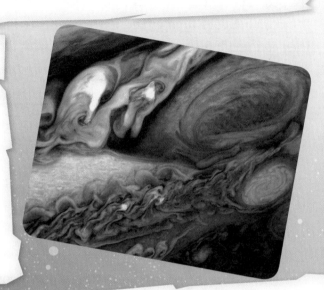

B Without our Sun we could not exist. Yes, that mighty orb that rises each morning and sets each night is vital to our existence on Earth. The Sun provides us with light, heat and energy. Without the Sun it would be so cold that no living thing on Earth could survive. Our planet would become a large ball of ice.

C Astronomers measure distance in space in light years. A light year is the distance that light can travel in one year. We know that light travels at around 300 000 kilometres per second in empty space. This means that, in one year, light travels 9 460 000 000 000 kilometres (9460 billion km). The nearest star to our solar system is about 4.3 light years away — that's about 40 678 000 000 000 kilometres (40 678 billion km).

D It may not feel like it, but we are all passengers on a very fast-moving vehicle. Earth is hurtling through space at 108 000 kilometres per hour. Considering there is a 110 km/h speed limit on our highways, that's pretty fast don't you think?

E More than a million meteors enter Earth's atmosphere every day! Luckily for us, most of them are only the size of a grain of sand and they burn up in the atmosphere, creating what we call 'shooting stars'. Those meteors that do reach Earth's surface are called 'meteorites'.

OXFORD UNIVERSITY PRESS

A paragraph usually (but not always) begins with a topic sentence.
The topic sentence is a sentence that lets us know the main idea of the paragraph.
The best topic sentences are those that get our attention and encourage us to read on.
The words at the start of a sentence can also provide topic links and help us predict how the text will unfold.

1 Write the five sentences you think are topic sentences from the text on page 52.

a _____

b _____

c _____

d _____

e _____

2 Use the topic sentences you have written above to shade the bubbles with the best answers.

a Paragraph A is about

○ giants   ○ the solar system   ○ Jupiter

b Paragraph B is about

○ the Sun   ○ the importance of the Sun   ○ light, heat and energy

c Paragraph C is about

○ astronomers   ○ measuring distance in space   ○ light years

d Paragraph D is about

○ passengers   ○ a fast-moving vehicle   ○ speed

e Paragraph E is about

○ meteors   ○ Earth's atmosphere   ○ shooting stars

CHALLENGE

On a separate piece of paper or on a computer, select one of the following topic sentences and write or type a paragraph of your own.

• Learning to draw cartoons can be fun.

• Although pets can be hard work, there are many rewards in owning at least one.

• There is nothing like the sight of a shark's fin cutting through the water to set the heart racing.

• My choice for a favourite sport may surprise you!

COMPARISONS

As wet as a fish — as dry as a bone;
As live as a bird — as dead as a stone;
As plump as a partridge — as poor as a rat;
As strong as a horse — as weak as a cat;
As hard as flint — as soft as a mole;
As white as a lily — as black as coal;
As plain as a staff — as rough as a bear;
As tight as a drum — as free as the air;
As heavy as lead — as light as a feather;
As steady as time — uncertain as weather;
As savage as tigers — as mild as a dove;
As stiff as a poker — as limp as a glove;
As blind as a bat — as deaf as a post;
As cool as a cucumber — as warm as toast;
As flat as a flounder — as round as a ball;
As blunt as a hammer — as sharp as an awl;
As brittle as glass — as tough as gristle;
As neat as a pin — as clean as a whistle;
As red as a rose — as square as a box;
As bold as a thief — as sly as a fox.

Anonymous

OXFORD UNIVERSITY PRESS

A simile is a group of words that compares two things.
The words *like* and *as* are used to begin similes.
For example: He flew **like a bird**. Our feet were **as cold as ice**.
The embarrassed performer turned **as red as a beetroot**.

Using similes can make your writing more interesting.

1 Use the poem to help you complete these similes.

a   as white as a _____

b   as warm as _____

c   as blind as a _____

d   as free as the _____

e   as limp as a _____

f   as round as a _____

g   as cool as a _____

h   as sly as a _____

i   as neat as a _____

j   as brittle as _____

k   as mild as a _____

l   as red as a _____

2 Use the poem to help you write T for True or F for False.

a   Tigers are savage. _____

b   A feather is light. _____

c   A flounder is round. _____

d   A lark is soft. _____

e   An awl is sharp. _____

f   Lead is light. _____

g   Coal is black. _____

h   A post cannot hear. _____

3 Use words or phrases from the box to complete these similes.

> the wind   a panther   a Cheshire cat   a knife through butter
> a monkey   a melon   a sore thumb   a bear with a sore head

a   She ran like _____.

b   The full moon was like _____.

c   After the team lost again the coach was like _____.

d   Martha entered the room grinning like _____.

e   Jack leapt from branch to branch like _____.

f   The new girl stuck out like _____.

g   Our teacher paced up and down the hallway like _____.

h   The canoe cut through the still waters like _____.

CHALLENGE

On a separate piece of paper or on a computer, write sentences that use these similes.

a   like jelly

b   as quick as a flash

c   as snug as a bug in a rug

d   like a tornado

Special places

The beach is a quarter of golden fruit,
a soft ripe melon
sliced to a half-moon curve,
having a thick green rind
of jungle growth;
and the sea devours it
with its sharp,
sharp white teeth.

William Hart-Smith

A place I like is the garage roof
Where the loquat leaves
All shiny and green
All polished and varnished
Make a shady screen
From grown-up eyes.

Our secret ship is the garage roof
Where the loquat leaves
Are the flags and sails
And the chicken coop
Is a great blue whale
With turquoise eyes.

Catherine Warry

OXFORD UNIVERSITY PRESS

A metaphor is a figure of speech in which one thing is compared to another. Although different, the things being compared share something in common.

For example: *The crocodile's teeth were white daggers.*
                 (Although not actually daggers, the crocodile's sharp teeth make the writer think of daggers.)

1 The poems on page 56 are strong in metaphors.

Use the poems to help you answer these questions.

What are the poets describing as:

> Writers use metaphors to make their descriptions more interesting and to entertain the reader.

a   a quarter of golden fruit? _____

b   a ship? _____

c   flags and sails? _____

d   thick green rind _____

e   a beast devouring a soft ripe melon? ___

f   a great blue whale? _____

_____

2 Use words in the box to complete these well-known metaphors.

steam	music	thorn	light
ants	journey	road hog	raging bull

a   Life is a _____ .

b   He's just letting off _____ .

c   That's _____ to my ears.

d   You are the _____ of my life.

e   The stormy sea was a _____ .

f   She's got _____ in her pants.

g   That opposition player is a _____ in our side.

h   The selfish driver was being a _____ .

CHALLENGE

Select one of the following to make metaphors of your own and then write one of them in an interesting sentence or poem of your own.

moon / balloon	lawn / carpet	classroom / zoo
snow / blanket	wind / howling dog	surfing / knife

This will be a piece of cake!

A

B

C

D

E

F

OXFORD UNIVERSITY PRESS

An idiom, like a metaphor, can be used to make what we write more interesting for the reader.

An idiom carries a different meaning from the actual words used.

For example: *to be a wet blanket* doesn't mean to cover oneself with a wet blanket but rather to be a spoilsport.

1 Choose letters from page 58 to match the cartoons with the idioms and their definitions shown below.

a   a piece of cake (something very easy to do) _____

b   a feather in the cap (to have done something one is proud of) _____

c   to sit on the fence (to not take sides in an argument or discussion) _____

d   to have a bee in your bonnet (to be preoccupied with something because you think it is very important) _____

e   to take the bull by the horns (to face and solve problems boldly) _____

f   to put the cart before the horse (to do things the wrong way around) _____

2 Underline the idioms that have been used in the following sentences.

a   "Don't shop there," said Rema, "you pay through the nose if you do."

b   After their argument the two friends eventually decided to bury the hatchet.

c   "I don't want to blow my own trumpet," boasted Paddy, 'but I'm the fastest runner at this school."

CHALLENGE

Here are some well-known idioms. Select two to write in sentences of your own.

to paddle one's own canoe (do things for oneself)

to turn over a new leaf (change the way things are done)

to get into hot water (to get into trouble)

to go down to the wire (to go to the very last minute before taking action)

_____

_____

_____

_____

Thunderstorms

Aboriginal and Islander creation stories

Creation stories are an extremely important part of many cultures around the world, including Aboriginal and Torres Strait Islander people.

These stories describe a period when human life began, when and how the land was shaped and when people were first set into their proper territories with the other living things that belonged in those places too. It was a time of blissful harmony between the Aboriginal and Islander people and their natural environment — a harmony that is still felt by many Indigenous people today. Because this period was a shape-changing time, when land features, weather patterns and the animals that exist, were formed, Australian Indigenous people see such things as part of their spirit and they hold them sacred.

In northern Australia, the Aboriginal and Torres Strait Islander people have many different stories to explain the furious thunderstorms that inevitably come each year with the wet season.

The Indigenous people of Arnhem Land believe that it is Jambuwal the thunder-man who, while travelling from place to place on large cumulus clouds, sheds torrential rain, which brings to life the earth below. Jambuwal's clouds contain the yurtus or spirit children who travel on the raindrops to earth where they look for a human mother to care for them.

On Melville Island, Bumerali strikes the ground with her great stone axe, creating frightening lightning flashes that can destroy trees and strike terrible fear into the hearts of the people below.

South of Arnhem Land, Mamaragan is the thunder-man. Like Jambuwal, Mamaragan lives in the wet-season clouds. The towering billows of these clouds are huge, white boulders. When the wet season comes, Mamaragan roars heartily with laughter and savagely beats the boulders together. His laughter is the rolling thunder, the sounds of the boulders striking each other is the crack of lightning and the sparks flying from those massive rocks form the flashes of lightning. The rain then tumbles towards the thirsty earth, giving life and food to the humans and all the other creatures dwelling below.

OXFORD UNIVERSITY PRESS

1 Underline the common nouns and circle the proper nouns in these sentences taken from the text on page 60.

a   On Melville Island, Bumerali strikes the ground with her axe creating lightning.

b   In northern Australia, the Aboriginal and Torres Strait Islander people have many different stories to explain the furious thunderstorms that inevitably come each year with the wet season.

c   South of Arnhem Land, Mamaragan is the thunder-man.

2 Which words in the following sentences are abstract nouns?

a   Bumerali strikes fear into the hearts of the people below. _____

b   It was a time of blissful harmony. _____

c   Australian Indigenous people see such things as part of their spirit. _____

3 Write a suitable adjective from the box to complete these sentences.

> white   torrential   towering   blissful   huge

a   In that time they lived in _____ harmony.

b   The _____ billows of these clouds are _____ boulders.

c   The clouds then shed _____ rain.

4 Which adverbs in the text best describe these verbs?

a   _____ beats

b   are _____ important

c   roars _____

5 Replace the repeated proper nouns in this sentence with suitable pronouns.
Bumerali strikes the ground with Bumerali's great stone axe when Bumerali is angry.

_____

_____

CHALLENGE

Write suitable synonyms for these words from the story on page 60.

a   big _____

b   hits _____

c   happy _____

TOPIC 3: ASSESS YOUR GRAMMAR!

Text cohesion and language devices

1 Shade the bubble next to an antonym for **tame**.

  ◯ wild   ◯ friendly   ◯ gentle   ◯ game

2 Shade the bubble next to the prefix that would make an antonym for **correct**.

  ◯ un-   ◯ dis-   ◯ im-   ◯ in-

3 Shade the bubble next to the suffix that could be used to change **thoughtful** to an antonym.

  ◯ -ness   ◯ -less   ◯ -ment   ◯ -ish

4 Shade the bubble next to a synonym for **lucky**.

  ◯ unlucky   ◯ plucky   ◯ luckily   ◯ fortunate

5 Shade the bubble next to the word that is *not* a synonym for **odd**.

  ◯ strange   ◯ peculiar   ◯ eccentric   ◯ ordinary

6 Shade the bubble next to the word that could replace the underlined words in this sentence.

Ratty and Mole found Ratty and Mole's way back to the riverbank.

  ◯ they   ◯ them   ◯ their   ◯ us

7 Shade the bubble next to the pronoun that could replace the underlined words in this sentence.

Riley took out twenty-eight footy cards and he laid the twenty-eight footy cards on the table.

  ◯ they   ◯ them   ◯ their   ◯ us

8 Write a suitable pronoun to complete this sentence.

I won the race so the victory is ⌒⎵⎵⎵⎵⎵⌒ .

OXFORD UNIVERSITY PRESS

9 Write a suitable relative pronoun to complete this sentence.

The flag (_____) was blue and yellow was placed at the top of the hill.

10 Write suitable time/sequence text connectives to complete these sentences.

(_____), place your right hand upon your head.

(_____), place your left hand on your right shoulder.

(_____), stand on one leg.

11 Shade the bubble next to the best answer. What do you think a paragraph beginning with the following topic sentence might be about?

Recently, the world has been rocked by several disastrous earthquakes, but what actually causes them?

○ the world   ○ disasters   ○ earthquakes   ○ how earthquakes occur

12 Shade the bubble next to the adjective that would best complete this simile.

as (_____) as an eel

○ eel-like   ○ wet   ○ slippery   ○ tasty

HOW AM I DOING?

Tick the boxes if you understand.

Using antonyms and synonyms can make my writing more interesting. ☐

Pronouns can stand in the place of nouns. ☐

Using language devices such as similes, metaphors and idioms can make my writing more entertaining for the reader. ☐

UNIT 4.1 Simple and compound sentences

An Iroquoian myth

Here is a story from the Native American Iroquoians.

Once, animals, plants and humans were friends.

The animals could speak in those days.

The three groups happily dwelt together.

Humans multiplied quickly.

The animals were pushed into the forests.

They were pushed into the deserts.

They were pushed into the seas.

Humans invented weapons.

They began to hunt the animals for food and clothing.

The animals were angry.

They decided to fight the humans.

Bear suggested the animals should use bows and arrows.

They could not use bows and arrows.

The animals decided to invent a new disease.

They would carry it.

When the humans hunted them, they would become infected.

They would become sick.

They might even die.

The plants were still friendly with the humans.

They decided to help them.

The plants allowed the humans to use them as remedies.

When humans became infected they consulted the plants.

The plants would then suggest a remedy.

That is how medicine came to the Iroquois.

OXFORD UNIVERSITY PRESS

A simple sentence has a noun or noun group (the subject), a verb and an object.

For example: *Seth kicked the ball.* (**Seth** is the subject, **kicked** is the verb, and **the ball** is the object.)

Compound sentences, however, are simple sentences joined together using a coordinating conjunction: *and, but, or* and *so*.

For example: *Seth kicked the ball* **but** *he missed the goal.*

CHALLENGE

The Iroquoian myth on page 64 has mostly been written using simple sentences. Written this way, it is quite uninteresting to read or enjoy.

Rewrite the myth using *and, so, but* and *or*, where necessary, to form compound sentences, making the story more pleasant for the audience to read.

For example: *Once, animals, plants and humans were friends. Animals could speak in those days and the three groups happily dwelt together.*

_____

_____

_____

_____

_____

_____

_____

_____

_____

_____

_____

_____

_____

_____

_____

_____

The lazy boy

There was a time, long ago, when the world was still growing.

In one tribe there lived a young boy who was a lazy and over-sleepy child. Everybody called him names and laughed at him.

When the men went hunting and fishing, the boy would secretly go to the sea and wash himself with magical herbs. Each day he became stronger and stronger but, when people came near him, he would pretend to be as lazy as usual.

There came a time when the tribe was threatened by the forest, which had decided to claim more land. It began to move from the mountains towards the sea, thereby crushing the settlements of the tribe.

The chiefs and medicine men had tried all of their magic powers to halt the forest without success. After a long council they decided that there was nothing for it — the people would have to abandon their villages and launch their canoes out to sea.

The lazy boy was disturbed by the ruckus of the people preparing their canoes. He asked why there was so much excitement. The chief scolded the boy and told him that if he had bothered to stay awake he would have been aware of the desperate plight of the tribe, and that whole villages had vanished while he had been sleeping.

The young man yawned then rose up and went to where the advancing forest had reached the outskirts of his village. There he began to pull up trees and with them he built a huge barricade.

He then pushed the barricade forwards, thereby sweeping the entire forest back into the hills from where it had come. Once there he pulled up more trees, roots and all, and he added to the barricade until it was so strong that there was little chance that the forest would ever move again.

The lazy boy returned to his village where he was welcomed as a hero, but he just yawned and said, "It is well that you only have such little things to worry you."

With that he curled up near the fire and went to sleep.

OXFORD UNIVERSITY PRESS

The **subject** of a sentence is the person or thing that the sentence is about.
For example: *The men were hunting.* subject = **the men**

The **verb** of a sentence tells us about the action or feelings of the subject.
For example: *The men were hunting.* verb = **were hunting**

The **subject** and **verb** of a sentence must agree. A singular subject must have a singular verb.
For example: *The man was hunting.*

A plural subject must have a plural verb. For example: *The men were hunting.*

1 When the **subject** is a pronoun, check carefully to make sure that the **subject** and **verb** agree. Use the table to help you decide which **verb** will best fit in the gaps in the following sentences.

a   I _____ leaving soon. (am, are, is)

b   We _____ having fun. (was, were)

c   They _____ dry clothes in their bags.
    (have, has)

d   He _____ wear glasses. (don't, doesn't)

e   It _____ swimming upstream. (was, were)

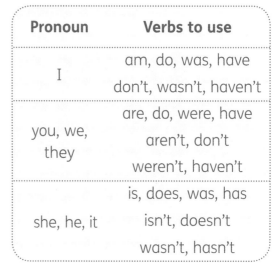

Pronoun	Verbs to use
I	am, do, was, have don't, wasn't, haven't
you, we, they	are, do, were, have aren't, don't weren't, haven't
she, he, it	is, does, was, has isn't, doesn't wasn't, hasn't

2 Circle the correct **verb**.

a   The world (was / were) growing.

b   The people must (prepare / prepares) their canoes.

c   Whole villages (had / has) vanished while he (were / was) sleeping.

d   The canoes (is / are) for escaping.

e   The lazy boy (were / was) disturbed by the ruckus.

f   The barricade (were / was) very strong.

g   The trees of the forest (was / were) advancing.

CHALLENGE

Collective nouns always have a singular verb. For example: *The forest of trees is advancing* NOT *The forest of trees are advancing.* Circle the correct **verb**.

a   The team (is / are) playing at home.

b   The flock of sheep (bleat / bleats) loudly.

c   The choir (was / were) singing beautifully.

d   A bunch of keys (was / were) hanging on the hook.

e   This pair of pants (is / are) too small.

f   The committee (is / are) meeting tomorrow.

Flash Flood

Something strange was happening in the mountains. A fat, black thunderstorm was brewing there and the clouds were swarming there and churning like vapour in a pot. The high blue hillsides had an angry scowl on top. Although the sun was shining on Even Stevens out on the plains, the ranges were heavy with shadow because the thundercaps were as dark and ugly as bruises. And then they started to let down streaks and streamers — dim and purple and blue-black — like long dark hair hanging from the sky. It was rain! Not a pitter-patter like a watering can; not a squirt like a sprinkler or the rose on a hose; but a crashing tumble like a million waterfalls. It hit the hard rocks on the tops of the ranges and raced down the sides; it bounced off the boulders and poured through the cracks; it tore down the hillsides, rushed into the gullies, and galloped for the gorges and the gaps. From all over the ranges the water streamed down. It spouted from every nook and channel. And the channels joined the gutters, the gutters joined the gullies and the gullies joined the valleys and the big deep creeks. Soon the water there was five feet deep, and then it was fifteen, and when you rubbed your eyes again it was fifty. It charged for the narrow gorges through the mountains like a million bullocks stampeding at a gate; it jostled with its shoulders and thundered with its head down and tore up rocks and boulders bigger than a car.

from *Flash Flood* by Colin Thiele

OXFORD UNIVERSITY PRESS

A coordinating conjunction is a joining word that links two phrases, adjectives or simple sentences together. The most common coordinating conjunctions are *and*, *but*, *so* and *or*.

For example: *I saw a blue train **and** a red tram.* (phrases joined)
                      *The children were wet **and** cold.* (adjectives joined)
                      *I am happy **but** Saffy is sad.* (simple sentences joined)

1 Use a coordinating conjunction (*and, but, so, or*) to rewrite these as one compound sentence.

a   A fat, black thunderstorm was brewing there. The clouds were swarming there and churning like vapour in a pot. _____

_____

b   It looked like long, dark hair. It was rain! _____

_____

c   Soon the water was five feet deep. Then it was fifteen. _____

_____

d   The surge was powerful. We ran for our lives. _____

_____

e   It was not a pitter-patter. It was a crashing tumble. _____

_____

f   We could stay here and watch. We could run for shelter. _____

_____

g   There was a thunderstorm brewing. We packed the car and left. _____

_____

2 Rewrite these sentences that have been joined with coordinating conjunctions as separate simple sentences.

a   The gutters joined the gullies and the gullies joined the valleys.

_____

b   It sounded like a million bullocks but it was really a torrent of water.

_____

CHALLENGE

Underline the coordinating conjunctions in these sentences.

a   The lamp burned low and flickering shadows danced on the walls.
b   The castaways were rescued but some had become very ill.
c   Cal and Cooper had behaved very well so Nikki bought them an ice cream each.
d   "You could wait here," said Max, "or you could wait over there if you prefer."

Join the joke!

when the two ghosts met in a dark alley

The elephant walked backwards into the telephone box.

when the elephant stampeded through the vineyard.

when he found the hunter fast asleep inside his tent

The famous composer hopped into his bath.

The bacon laughed.

We went to the cannibal's wedding.

The car blushed.

when Harry complained that he felt like a curtain

when Detective Andy Ware stopped two robbers, Calvin and Klein, at the bank door

Conjunctions

because   when   where

He immediately knew that he had caught a pair of nickers.

The grapes gave out a little wine.

The tiger said, "Yummy, breakfast in bed!"

It was love at first fright.

because the traffic lights were changing

when the egg cracked a yolk

The doctor told him to pull himself together.

where he wrote a soap opera

because he wanted to reverse the charges

where they toasted the bride and groom

OXFORD UNIVERSITY PRESS

Complex sentences are formed when we join a main clause with a subordinate clause.

A main clause can stand on its own as a sentence. For example: *The bacon laughed.*

A subordinate clause cannot stand as a sentence on its own. For example: *when the egg cracked a yolk*

We join subordinate clauses to main clauses with subordinating conjunctions such as *because, when, where.*

For example: *The bacon laughed **when** the egg cracked a yolk.*

OR   ***When** the egg cracked a yolk, the bacon laughed.*

1 You will notice that on page 70 the main clauses of the jokes are uncoloured and the subordinate clauses are coloured. Join the jokes by rewriting them as complex sentences. Write the subordinating conjunction that has been used to link the two clauses of each joke.

For example: *The bacon laughed when the egg cracked a yolk.*   when

> Subordinating conjunctions can begin sentences.

a _____

_____

b _____

_____

c _____

_____

d _____

_____

e _____

_____

f _____

_____

g _____

_____

h _____

_____

i _____

_____

j _____

_____

The children of the Sun

Myths, legends and folk tales are stories that have been passed down from generation to generation. They are the ways in which the people from some cultures explain the world around them.

Here is a tale from West Africa that explains why there is only one sun in the sky.

Long ago, when the world was only new, the daylight was much stronger than it is today.

The people who lived on Earth could not come out during the day because it was too bright and too hot. The Sun sat in the sky as he does today, but in the sky with him were his many brilliant children.

The Moon also sat in the sky surrounded by her many children, but they were no problem for the people on Earth because the Moon only shone at night and her children were pale compared to the Sun's children.

The people complained to the Moon, telling her how difficult it was to only be able to gather food at night and to live in fear of going blind in the brightness of the day.

After listening patiently for a long time, the Moon felt sorry for the people, so she decided to help them.

At the time when the Moon is dropping below the horizon and the Sun is rising in the east, the Moon spoke to the Sun. She told the Sun that she was worried that their children, both of the night and the day, were causing problems for the Earth people and perhaps some of them should be sent away.

The Moon took up a huge sack and began filling it with white pebbles, pretending that she was gathering up her pale children. When the Sun saw what the Moon was doing, he gathered up all of his own bright and hot children and shoved them into a sack.

Together the Moon and the Sun took their full sacks to the lake and tossed them in.

Later that night the Sun became angry when he realised that he had been tricked by the Moon. The next morning he rushed to the lake to retrieve his children. He could see them glistening just below the gently rippling surface of the water. When he scooped up one of his children and lifted it from the water, it gulped and died. The same thing happened with the next child and the next, until the Sun realised that he would never be able to retrieve his children from the lake. He sadly returned to the sky.

Today the Sun's children still live in the lake, but rather than blinding people with their brightness they dart about all shimmering and gleaming below the rippling waters — as fish.

OXFORD UNIVERSITY PRESS

Complex sentences use subordinating conjunctions to join a main clause with a subordinate clause. Each clause has a verb. For example: *The game won't start **until** the rain stops.*

A main clause can stand on its own as a sentence. For example: *The game won't start.*

A subordinate clause cannot stand as a sentence on its own. For example: *until the rain stops*

We join subordinate clauses to main clauses with subordinating conjunctions such as *because, when, where, until, after, before, since, as, unless, although.*

1 Rewrite the following main clauses and subordinate clauses as complex sentences.

Underline the subordinating conjunctions in each complex sentence.

a Long ago the daylight was much stronger than it is today. when the world was only new

_____

_____

b The Moon felt sorry for the people. after listening patiently for a long time

_____

_____

c The Moon's many children were no problem for the people on Earth. because the Moon only shone at night_____

_____

d Today the Sun's children still live in the lake. where they dart about all shimmering and gleaming _____

_____

2 Choose a subordinating conjunction from the box to join these clauses.

a We will get the best seats in the stadium _____ someone gets there first.

b _____ our pet duck died the drake has been very sad and lonely.

c The children ate lunch _____ they entered the museum.

d _____ we have sent several emails there has been no reply.

e Our scout troop pitched a tent _____ Cobra Troop gathered firewood.

until
before
since
when
unless
after
while
although

CHALLENGE

Circle the verbs or verb groups in each clause in question 2 above.

You can quote me!

The newsreader announced that following a collision between a prison van and a cement mixer, police were looking for six hardened criminals.

The politician declared that if the government didn't succeed with its new plan then it ran the risk of failure.

At the pre-season training camp, the football coach had told his boys that they should think of one word and one word only for the entire season, and that word was Grand Final.

Seven days without laughter makes one weak!

A day without sunshine is like ... night.

If everybody thinks alike ... somebody isn't thinking.

OXFORD UNIVERSITY PRESS

Quoted (direct) speech shows words that are actually spoken.

For example: *"Throw the ball to me," yelled Tina.*

We show quoted (direct) speech by using speech marks (also called talking marks or quotation marks). In the example above, the actual words spoken are *Throw the ball to me.*

1 Underline the quoted (direct) speech.

a "Could I please have some more?" asked Oliver.

b "If everybody minded their own business," the Duchess said in a hoarse growl, "the world would go round a great deal faster than it does."

c "You have nice manners for a thief and liar," said the dragon.

d "Mother!" yelled Charlie, rushing in on them like a hurricane. "Look! I've got it! Look, Mother, look! The last Golden Ticket! It's mine!"

2 Read the texts on page 74 and write them as quoted (direct) speech.

a _____

said the newsreader _____

b _____ said Merv.

c _____

_____ said the football coach.

d _____ said the politician _____

_____

e _____ said Mort.

f _____ said Mary.

_____

You can enclose spoken words with speech marks in four ways:

• by using the spoken words only: *"Are you ready yet?"*

• by using unspoken words to introduce spoken words: *Will asked, "Are you ready yet?"*

• by using unspoken words after the spoken words: *"Are you ready yet?" asked Will.*

• and by separating the spoken words: *"Are you ready yet?" asked Will. "We'll be late if you don't hurry."*

3 Write the following as quoted (direct) speech using the correct punctuation where necessary.

a Phil told me that he would arrive at 4 o'clock. _____

_____

b I was asked by my teacher to list my favourite films. _____

_____

CHALLENGE

On a separate piece of paper or on a computer, write or type a conversation between yourself and an alien, using quoted (direct) speech. Explain to him or her how to play a game. Imagine that the alien is having trouble understanding you but is very curious to know about the game.

How the tortoise got his shell

Zeus, the king of the gods, decided to invite all of the animals to his wedding feast. He announced that he would be honoured if all of the animals of the forest would attend his celebration.

On the day of the wedding, the tortoise told his wife that he would rather stay at home than go to Zeus's feast.

At the feast, Zeus noticed that tortoise was absent. He asked squirrel if tortoise was too ill to have accepted the god's invitation. The squirrel told Zeus that as far as she knew tortoise was quite well.

The next day Zeus went to the hollow tree in the forest where tortoise lived. He asked tortoise why he had not attended the wedding feast with all the other forest animals. The tortoise answered that he liked no better place than his own home.

Zeus angrily told the tortoise that he would pay for his laziness and ill manners.

With a crash of thunder and a flash of lightning, Zeus magically placed a shell-house upon the tortoise's back, and tortoise has carried his home on his back ever since.

retold from Aesop by AjW

Quoted (direct) speech is used to show words that are actually spoken.

For example: **"Tell me a story or I'll gobble you up,"** *growled the giant.*

Reported (indirect) speech shows what has been said without using the exact words.

For example: *The giant told Jack that* **if he didn't tell him a story then he would gobble him up**.

The story on page 76 has been written in reported (indirect) speech.

Rewrite the story on the lines below using quoted (direct) speech where necessary.

a   Zeus, the king of the gods, decided to invite all of the animals to his wedding feast.

_____

_____

_____

b   At the feast, Zeus noticed that tortoise was absent.

_____

_____

_____

_____

c   The next day Zeus went to the hollow tree in the forest where tortoise lived.

_____

_____

_____

_____

d   With a crash of thunder and a flash of lightning, Zeus magically placed a shell-house upon the tortoise's back, and tortoise has carried his home on his back ever since.

_____

_____

_____

_____

CHALLENGE

On a separate piece of paper or on a computer, rewrite or type this joke using the correct punctuation.

a boy walks into a shop with a pig under his arm mr Collins, the manager, spots him and says thats the ugliest looking animal ive ever seen where did you get it I won it at a raffle answers the pig

Let's laugh at some limericks!

I'd rather have fingers than toes,
I'd rather have ears than a nose.
And as for my hair,
I'm glad it's all there,
I'll be awfully sad when it goes.

An elderly fellow named Keith,
Mislaid his set of false teeth.
They'd been laid on his chair,
He'd forgotten them there,
He sat down and was bitten beneath.

A young gourmet dining at Crewe,
Found a rather large mouse in his stew.
Said the waiter, "Don't shout,
And wave it about,
Or they'll all be wanting one too."

A canner, exceedingly canny,
One morning remarked to his granny,
"A canner can can
Anything that he can,
But a canner can't can a can, can he?"

If you're lacking a little good cheer,
Go and tickle a bull on his ear.
For I'm sure that the rumour,
That they've no sense of humour,
Is merely a product of fear.

TICKLE
TICKLE

OXFORD UNIVERSITY PRESS

An **apostrophe of contraction** is used to show that a letter has (or letters have) been left out.

For example: *I'm = I am*   *can't = can not*   *we've = we have*

1 Write these **contractions** in full.

a   I've = _____

b   what's = _____

c   couldn't = _____

d   it's = _____

e   here's = _____

f   doesn't = _____

g   wasn't = _____

h   we're = _____

i   he'd = _____ **or** _____

j   she's = _____ **or** _____

k   he's = _____ **or** _____

l   I'd = _____ **or** _____

> The contraction *it's* always means 'it is' or 'it has'.
> For example:
> It's over there.
> It's been snowing.
> The contraction *who's* always means 'who is' or 'who has'.
> For example: Who's knocking at my door?
> Who's been knocking on my door?
> The word *whose* shows that someone possesses something.
> For example: Whose dog is this?

2 Use an **apostrophe of contraction** and shorten these words.

a   is not _____

b   they had _____

c   we had _____

d   they have _____

e   I have _____

f   did not _____

g   they are _____

h   I will _____

i   that is _____

j   must not _____

k   she has _____

l   he is _____

3 Rewrite the sentences using **apostrophes of contraction** to shorten words where possible.

a   "I am going to the lifesavers' practice at Dolphin Point on Sunday," said Todd. _____

_____

_____

b   You can not go into the hall if the door is not open. _____

_____

c   We are packed and ready to leave. _____

_____

d   She is the fastest runner in the class. _____

_____

CHALLENGE

On a separate piece of paper or on a computer, write or type in full all of the **contractions** you can find in the limericks on page 78.

Heroes and villains

Preppo Boy

Power Girl

Veronica Vile

Dr Eveel

Erik the Viking

Spruce Sprocket

cape of invisibility

hammer

freeze ring

shrink powder

super spy glass

energy gloves

OXFORD UNIVERSITY PRESS

An apostrophe of possession is used to show that something is owned by someone or something.

For example: The dog's paw (The paw of the dog)
                 The team's victory (The victory of the team)
                 The tree's leaves (The leaves of the tree)   **but**
                 The trees' leaves (The leaves of the trees)

1 There are six comic-book characters shown on page 80. Match each character with the 'instruments of trade' inside the bag at the bottom of the page that you think best suit them. There are no 'correct' answers but remember to use apostrophes of possession to show ownership.

a _____ energy gloves   b_____ freeze ring

c _____ shrink powder   d _____ super spy glass

e _____ cape of invisibility   f _____ hammer

2 Rewrite these phrases using apostrophes of possession.

a   the wings of the bird _____

b   the noise of the city _____

c   the scream of the chainsaw _____

d   the verandah of the house _____

e   the songs of the performers _____

> If a noun is plural and already ends in s, to show possession add an *apostrophe* of possession but no s. For example: the boys' caps (the caps belonging to the boys); the boy's caps (the caps belonging to the boy)

3 Rewrite the following using apostrophes of possession where necessary.

a   The cars horn warned the cyclist in the nick of time. _____
   _____

b   My sisters wallet lay open and empty on the table._____
   _____

c   The soldiers weapon was leaning against a nearby tree. _____
   _____

d   We could hear the cats meow coming from deep inside the drain. _____
   _____

CHALLENGE

On a separate piece of paper or on a computer, continue this sports report, using at least five more apostrophes of possession.

The game began at the Sharks' home ground, with the Dolphins' captain winning the toss. The first goal of the game came at the forty-second mark when Robinson's pass found Bennet in the Sharks' goal square. Bennet's kick was ...

Hooley dooley, that was no dolphin!

While surfing on his own, Lockie Leonard has been suddenly entertained by a pod of dolphins playfully skylarking around him.

Then, in one strange second they all peeled off, dived and were gone. In the long lull between sets, Lockie waited, still hopeful that they'd return and stir up some more fun. But nothing happened. With all the excitement gone he suddenly felt his aching body. He'd been surfing for hours and even his pains had pains and his rashes had rashes. He could feel the end of his nose shrivelling under its coating of zinc cream. What a shame they took off, he thought. I could've handled an hour of that.

Just as he was thinking it, he saw a shadow turning in the swell. Yes! And as a small set rose in the distance, Lockie saw the dolphin's fin pop from the crest of the first wave.

Then he stopped paddling.

Lockie sat up. He stared again. Hard. His heart went small and cold as a leftover rissole inside his Rip Curl vest. Because, you see, as any grommet knows, there are fins and there are FINS!

There it was again.

Hooley dooley, that was no dolphin. Lockie Leonard was no brain surgeon but he knew the difference between 'Flipper' and 'Jaws III'. It was a Noah's ark. A man in a grey flannel suit. The fish with the tax collector's smile. A swimming lawyer. Five rows of teeth with a tail, an appetite and a seriously bad attitude. In short, it was a cartilaginous fish characterised by a pointed snout extending forward and over a crescentic mouth set with sharp triangular teeth, a creature quite necessary to the fine balance of the marine environment but not particularly welcomed by hairy young persons floating on tiny pieces of fibreglass in the middle of the cold, lonely ocean. It was in fact, a S S S H H H H A A A A A A R K!

from *Lockie Leonard: Legend* by Tim Winton

OXFORD UNIVERSITY PRESS

1 Write whether the following sentences are simple or compound sentences.

a Lockie sat up. _____

b It was a Noah's ark. _____

c He'd been surfing for hours and even his pains had pains. _____

d Hooley dooley, that was no dolphin. _____

e Lockie was no brain surgeon but he knew the difference between 'Flipper' and

'Jaws III'. _____

2 Circle the correct verbs in each of these sentences so that the subject and verb agree.

a They all peeled off, dived and (was / were) gone.

b As any young grommet knows, there (is / are) fins and there (is / are) FINS.

c Just as he (were / was) thinking it, he (saw / seen) a shadow turning in the swell.

3 Rewrite the following from the text on page 82 as if Lockie was saying rather than thinking it. Don't forget your punctuation.

What a shame they took off, he thought. I could've handled an hour of that.

_____

_____

_____

_____

CHALLENGE

1 Write these contractions in full.

a could've _____   b wasn't _____   c they'd _____

2 Rewrite the following using an apostrophe of possession where it belongs.

a a Noahs ark _____

b the dolphins fin _____

c the tax collectors smile _____

TOPIC 4: ASSESS YOUR GRAMMAR!

Clauses, conjunctions, sentences and punctuation

1 Shade the bubble next to the simple sentence.

○ It is against the law to kill snakes in Victoria because they are protected.

○ Oscar and Lucy like playing basketball.

○ When the cold southerly wind begins to blow, you know winter has arrived.

○ He slammed on the brakes and the car skidded to a halt.

2 Shade the bubble that shows the coordinating conjunction in this compound sentence.

We finally reached the station but the train had already departed.

○ We ○ reached ○ but ○ had

3 Shade the bubble that shows the coordinating conjunction in this compound sentence.

The Rainbow Serpent slithered across the land and then he disappeared into the gullies.

○ slithered ○ across ○ and ○ carved

4 Shade the bubble next to the best coordinating conjunction to join these two sentences.

Night was beginning to fall. We decided to pitch our tent.

○ and ○ so ○ but ○ or

5 Shade the bubble next to the best coordinating conjunction to join these two sentences.

The footballer was hoping to be selected in the team. The coach told him he was not yet fit enough.

○ and ○ so ○ but ○ or

6 Shade the bubble next to the word that would best complete this sentence.

The people _____ gathered at the dock awaiting the sailor's return.

○ was ○ were ○ is ○ am

OXFORD UNIVERSITY PRESS

7 Shade the bubble next to the word that would best complete this sentence.

They _____ returned from overseas.

○ am   ○ has   ○ have   ○ is

8 Shade the bubble next to the subordinating conjunction that would best complete this complex sentence.

The Sun became angry _____ he realised the Moon had tricked him.

○ since   ○ unless   ○ where   ○ when

9 Write the words actually spoken in the following quoted (direct) speech.

"If you're coming," called Bryce, "you'd better hurry up!"

[ ]

10 Write the following as quoted (direct) speech.

The tourist asked where the museum was located.

[ ]

11 Shade the bubble next to the correct contraction of **you are**.

○ your   ○ you're   ○ your'e   ○ youre'

12 Shade the bubble that shows the correct use of the apostrophe of possession.

the steeples of the churches

○ the church's steeples   ○ the church'es steeples

○ the churche's steeples   ○ the churches' steeples

HOW AM I DOING?

Tick the boxes if you understand.

I can identify simple and compound sentences. [ ]

Apostrophes of contraction can be used to shorten words. [ ]

Apostrophes of possession show ownership. [ ]

Quotation or speech marks show the actual words spoken. [ ]

Do plants cry?

Some botanists believe that plants have the same emotions as humans. They also believe that plants know their enemies and react badly when a threat approaches.

The botanist Cleve Backster attempted an experiment on a philodendron, because he wanted to measure how quickly water rose from the root system to the leaves. He decided to use an instrument called a polygraph (lie detector), because it can be used to measure electrical resistance. To his surprise, when wired up, the plant showed the same emotional stimulation that a human might show if wired to a similar machine.

Being curious, as all scientists should be, Backster decided that he would attempt to get a different reaction from the plant by burning one of its leaves. However, while he was thinking about this, the plant showed an incredible reading on the polygraph. Without actually touching the plant, Backster had 'frightened the life out of it' when he thought about burning its leaves.

You may be reluctant now about gulping down your dinner tonight, because the thought of screaming cabbages or moaning mashed potatoes upsets you. However, there is no need to be concerned. To date, no one has been able to produce positive evidence that a cornstalk weeps uncontrollably when you rip off that delicious corn cob and take it to your dinner table.

Cleve Backster with his polygraph (lie detector)

OXFORD UNIVERSITY PRESS

Informative texts such as explanations use paragraphs to organise information. The first paragraph in an information report often starts with a topic sentence identifying what is being explained. The following paragraphs provide an explanation in sequence.

1 Read 'Do plants cry?'. Write the topic sentence used to introduce the explanation.

_____

_____

Complex sentences with subordinating conjunctions (joining main clauses with subordinate clauses) often feature in explanations. The subordinating conjunction *because* is commonly found in explanations, because the purpose of explanations is to explain how something happens or why something occurs.

For example: *Some botanists believe plants have emotions* **because** *they have read about an experiment by Cleve Backster.*

2 Underline the subordinating conjunctions in these complex sentences.

  a The plants showed the same emotional stimulation as humans when wired up to the polygraph machine.

  b You may be reluctant about gulping down your dinner tonight, because the thought of screaming cabbages is disturbing.

  c When Backster thought about burning the plant's leaves, the plant showed a strong response on the polygraph.

3 Use coordinating conjunctions (*and, but, or, so*) to rewrite these simple sentences as compound sentences.

  a Plants know their enemies. They react when a threat approaches. _____

  _____

  b You may be reluctant. There is no need to be. _____

  _____

Technical or scientific nouns often feature in explanation texts. For example: *polygraph*

4 Write three more examples of technical nouns used in the explanation text on page 86.

_____

CHALLENGE

Which text connective links the sentence about Backster's idea to burn the plant's leaves to the reaction the plant had to this?

_____

Trunchbull

"You!" the Trunchbull shouted, pointing a finger the size of a rolling-pin at a boy called Wilfred. Wilfred was on the extreme right of the front row.

"Stand up, you!" she shouted at him.

Wilfred stood up.

"Recite the three-times table backwards!" the Trunchbull barked.

"Backwards?" stammered Wilfred. "But I haven't learnt it backwards."

"There you are!" cried Trunchbull, triumphant. "She's taught you nothing! Miss Honey, why have you taught them absolutely nothing at all in the last week?"

"That's not true, Headmistress," Miss Honey said. "They have all learnt their three-times table. But I see no point in teaching it to them backwards. There is little point in teaching anything backwards. The whole object of life, Headmistress, is to go forwards. I venture to ask whether even you, for example, can spell a simple word like **wrong** backwards straight away. I very much doubt it."

"Don't you get impertinent with me, Miss Honey!" the Trunchbull snapped, then she turned back to the unfortunate Wilfred. "Very well, boy," she said. "Answer me this. I have seven apples, seven oranges and seven bananas. How many pieces of fruit do I have altogether? Hurry up! Get on with it! Give me the answer!"

"That's **adding up!**" Wilfred cried. "That isn't the three-times table!"

"You blithering idiot!" shouted the Trunchbull. "You festering gumboil! You fleabitten fungus! That is the three-times table! You have three separate lots of fruit and each lot has seven pieces. Three sevens are twenty-one. Can't you see that, you stagnant cesspool! I'll give you one more chance. I have eight coconuts, eight monkey-nuts and eight nutty little idiots like you. How many nuts do I have altogether? Answer me quickly."

Poor Wilfred was properly flustered. "Wait!" he cried. "Please wait! I've got to add up eight coconuts and eight monkey-nuts ..." He started counting on his fingers.

"You bursting blister!" yelled the Trunchbull. "You moth-eaten maggot! This is not adding up! This is multiplication! The answer is three eights! Or is it eight threes? What is the difference between three eights and eight threes? Tell me that, you mangled little wurzel and look sharp about it!"

By now Wilfred was far too frightened and bewildered to even speak.

from *Matilda* by Roald Dahl

OXFORD UNIVERSITY PRESS

Imaginative texts, like this extract from *Matilda* by Roald Dahl, often feature quoted (direct) speech using quotation marks to show what is actually being said. Narratives like this often use a new line for quoted speech to show that someone else is now speaking.

1 Read 'Trunchbull' then rewrite the following so they are correctly punctuated. Don't forget to use quotation marks where needed.

a   stand up you she shouted at him _____

_____

b   miss honey why havent you taught them anything this week yelled trunchbull _____

_____

c   I don't know them backwards stammered wilfred I only know them forwards _____

_____

Clever authors, like Roald Dahl, often use precise saying verbs to develop a particular impression of characters.

For example: *"Recite the three-times table backwards!" the Trunchbull **barked**. "Backwards?"*
                            ***stammered** Wilfred.*

2 Write the saying verbs used by the author to develop each of these characters.

a   The Trunchbull: _____

b   Wilfred: _____

c   Miss Honey: _____

Metaphors can be used very effectively in narratives. Metaphors make a direct comparison.

As readers, we build an impression of the Trunchbull as a really nasty character from the cruel metaphors she uses to describe Wilfred.

For example: *"You festering gumboil! You fleabitten fungus!"*

3 Write four more metaphors used by the Trunchbull to describe Wilfred.

_____

_____

CHALLENGE

Which punctuation mark has Roald Dahl used effectively to emphasise the character

of the Trunchbull? Explain your answer. _____

_____

_____

Adverb Man – Metamorphosis

Connor has written a review for the school magazine to persuade readers to see the new *Adverb Man* movie.

Last Saturday afternoon, I was lucky enough to attend the premiere of the latest Adverb Man movie, **Adverb Man – Metamorphosis**. Wow! I was absolutely blown away!

Not only is this movie packed with exciting, mind-boggling, death-defying stunts and special effects, it is also a real hoot! This movie will have you laughing in the aisles! It was weird leaving the cinema and seeing everybody in the same condition as me, with tears streaming down their cheeks.

The main character, superhero and all-round good guy, Adverb Man (played hilariously by Dustbin Hoffmun) bungles his way to somehow saving the heroine, Maddy Heaven (Sheryl Peep), from the clutches of the evil and torturously incompetent but funny bad guy, Kevin (Kisstofer Walkman). Next, our hero turns his attention to using (or perhaps 'misusing' would be a better term) his fantastic but unreliable superpowers to save Earth from an imminent collision with an intergalactic, giant caterpillar. Yes folks, you have read correctly – a caterpillar hurtling through space, threatening billions of humans with extinction.

I won't be a spoilsport and reveal just how A-Man solves this collision problem but the subtitle of the movie may give you a clue.

In summary, this is a fantastic movie – certainly much more entertaining than last year's **Adverb Man – The Beginning**. I suggest you raid your piggy banks as soon as possible, grab a ticket and get along to your local cinema for a wonderful couple of hours of very funny and action-packed entertainment. You won't be disappointed! This is definitely a movie you must see!

OXFORD UNIVERSITY PRESS

Reviews use a lot of evaluative language to give a positive or negative opinion. This is often in the form of adjectives that offer the writer's opinion. If the writer gives a positive opinion of the movie, the reader is often persuaded to see the movie (or read the book).

For example: *excellent* (positive opinion), *boring* (negative opinion)

1 Read the film review. Does the writer give a positive or negative opinion?

_____

2 Write six adjectives from the review that give the writer's opinion.

_____

_____

Persuasive texts often use modal verbs and modal adverbs with a high degree of certainty.

For example: *This movie* **will** *definitely rate in the top three for this year.*

3 Underline the modal verbs in these sentences.

   a   This movie will end soon.   b   You should see this movie!

   c   I could watch this again.   d   You might want to take a friend.

4 Underline the modal adverb in these sentences.

   a   This is certainly a movie that will suit all ages.

   b   I always enjoy the Adverb Man movies.

   c   This movie is absolutely hilarious.

The use of noun groups with a wide range of adjectives can be used in a review to provide a fuller description of characters, events and incidents.

5 Write the noun group used in the review for each of the following nouns.

   a   (stunts) _____

   b   (Kevin) _____

   c   (caterpillar) _____

   d   (Adverb Man) _____

   e   (superpowers) _____

CHALLENGE

On a separate piece of paper or on a computer, write or type your own persuasive text in the form of a review of a movie you have recently seen, your favourite book, a computer game you like to play or some music you would like to recommend. Include modal verbs and adverbs and interesting noun groups. Finish your review with a concluding paragraph which gives a judgement that includes a positive or negative opinion.

Sharks, snakes and spiders

White pointer

The white pointer, also known as the great white, is the most feared of sharks. Its name comes from its white underside, which contrasts with its dark grey or blue-grey back.

The white pointer, which can measure up to 11 metres, has a frightful reputation as a man-eater. It is believed that most attacks by the white pointer occur when the shark thinks that it is attacking its usual prey: seals and sea lions.

Taipan

The taipan has a large rectangular-shaped head, narrow neck, cylindrical body and red eyes. The taipan, a master at hunting, strikes with amazing speed, more than once in some cases, and then waits for its prey to die from its venom.

When approached by humans, the snake is alert and nervous. If it feels threatened, the snake becomes extremely dangerous. The preferred prey of the taipan is birds, mice, bandicoots and lizards.

Tiger snake

The tiger snake has a flat, blunt head with a strong, robust body. The colour of the snake can range from brown, grey and olive to green, with lighter crossbands of creamy yellow.

The snake eats birds, small mammals, lizards and even fish, although frogs are its preferred prey. Tiger snakes, one of the world's deadliest creatures, are abundant throughout south-eastern Australia, making them a feared snake to humans living in that area.

Blue shark

This fast, beautiful, slender shark gets its name from the deep-blue colour of its back. A swift, graceful, streamlined hunter, the blue shark is one of the most commonly seen sharks.

Funnel-web spider

The funnel-web, a large spider, lives on the ground or in trees. The spider is blue-black, purple-black or dark grey in colour.

To bite, the funnel-web raises the front of its body, and its front legs, off the ground. Venom from this spider can be fatal to humans. If bitten, apply a pressure bandage and seek medical help.

Redback spider

The redback is a small, black, web-spinning spider. The female, which can harm humans, has a large, red spot on her back.

The redback spins a tangled, sticky, untidy web, which is extremely strong and has been known to trap insects, both large and small, lizards and even small mammals.

A rogues' gallery?

tiger snake	taipan
wolf spider	funnel-web spider
tarantula	blue shark
redback spider	hammerhead shark
white pointer shark	copperhead
eastern brown snake	shortfin mako shark
red-bellied black snake	grey nurse shark
cobra	black widow spider
tiger shark	

OXFORD UNIVERSITY PRESS

The comma is used:

a   to show a pause in a sentence.

For example: *The white pointer, also known as the great white, is the most feared of sharks.*

b   to separate adjectives that describe one noun.

For example: *We sat beside the cool, clear, sparkling waters of the lake.*

c   to separate the words in a list.

For example: *In my bag I carried marbles, lollies, trading cards, an old banana and my homework.*

d   to separate a main clause and a subordinate clause.

For example: *The giant, who had not yet seen the children, carried on counting the gold coins.*

1 Read 'Sharks, snakes and spiders'. Circle any commas separating lists of nouns or adjectives. Use a different colour to highlight the remaining commas.

2 Write commas where they belong in these sentences.

a   The funnel-web a large spider lives on the ground or in trees.

b   A swift graceful streamlined hunter the blue shark is one of the most commonly seen sharks.

c   The redback spider traps insects lizards and small mammals.

d   The white pointer also known as the great white is the most feared of sharks.

e   The redback is a small black web-spinning spider.

f   If bitten apply a pressure bandage and seek medical help.

g   The redback spins a tangled sticky untidy web.

h   The snake eats birds small mammals lizards and even fish although frogs are its preferred prey.

i   Alert and nervous when approached by humans the snake is extremely dangerous when threatened.

> Without commas, our writing could cause a great deal of confusion.
> For example: For today only, Year 5 kids are on yard duty.
> For today, only Year 5 kids are on yard duty.

CHALLENGE

Use the 'rogues' gallery' opposite to complete the following sentences.
Don't forget to use commas where necessary.

a   The world's most dangerous sharks include the white pointer _____

_____

b   The world's most dangerous snakes include the taipan _____

_____

c   The world's most dangerous spiders include the funnel-web _____

_____

Homonym headlines

a

Doctors losing ****

b

Death of another packet of Cornflakes – Police searching for **** killer.

c

Gardener has difficulty finding **** in messy garage.

d

Newly copied scientist says, "Clones are people, ****!"

e

Plumber finds that water leaking through roof is a **** problem.

f

Glazier graduates as doctor, visits patients in hospital with broken window and promises to fix ****.

g

Vet finds foal has raspy whinny because he is a little ****.

h

Aquarium soon to close down. Keeper lets out big ****.

i

Cook's running out of ****!

j

Bakers **** more dough!

k

Hungry mother of 13 used penknife to cut cake because she only wanted a little ****.

l

Guests told that their **** would be enough at Prince's birthday bash.

OXFORD UNIVERSITY PRESS

Homonyms can be divided into two groups. **Homophones** sound the same but are spelled differently and have different meanings. For example: *pale* (a light colour), *pail* (a bucket)

Homographs are words that are spelled the same but have different meanings.
For example: *saw* (past tense of *see*), *saw* (a tool)

1 The headlines on page 94 aren't complete. Write the missing pairs of words using the homonyms in the box below.

For example: *Cook's running out of **time**. (a measure of seconds, minutes, days, etc.)*

   *Cook's running out of **thyme**. (a herb)* i = time, thyme

ceiling	cereal	hoes	thyme	patients	horse	knead	piece
two	wail	pain	pane	time	serial	peace	presence
sealing	hose	patience	whale	too	need	hoarse	presents

a _____   b _____

c _____   d _____

e _____   f _____

g _____   h _____

i   *time, thyme* _____   j _____

k _____   l _____

2 Write homophones for the following words.

a   break _____   b   rays _____   c   allowed _____   d   suite _____

e   weigh _____   f   coarse _____   g   bold _____   h   heard _____

i   creek _____   j   hole _____   k   sail _____   l   sell _____

3 Write the different meanings for these homographs.

a   bank _____

b   fan _____

CHALLENGE

Some homographs are spelled the same but they have different meanings and they sound different. For example: *lead* (rhymes with *feed*) means to *guide*   *lead* (rhymes with *fed*) means *metal*. Write homographs to match these meanings.

a   water produced when crying / pulls apart _____

b   a female pig / to scatter seed _____

c   pull with oars / a noisy quarrel _____

d   the front of a ship / to bend at the waist / a stringed weapon / a knot with a double loop _____

NAIDOC Week

The word NAIDOC is an **acronym**. An acronym is a word or name formed from the initial letters of a phrase or title. NAIDOC stands for National Aborigines and Islander Day Observance Committee.

When is NAIDOC Week?

Originally the NAIDOC celebration was for only one day, as the acronym suggests. These days, however, the celebration lasts for one full week, usually beginning on the first Sunday of July each year.

How did NAIDOC Week start?

On 26 January 1938, to protest the white celebration of what was seen as the invasion of Australia by Europeans, Aboriginal rights groups marched through the streets of Sydney. The day of that protest became known as the Day of Mourning and many Aboriginal people still boycott what has become known as Australia Day.

In 1955 the Day of Mourning was moved to the first Sunday in July and, in 1975, the decision was made to make NAIDOC events and celebrations last for an entire week.

Why does the NAIDOC celebration last a whole week?

Once a day of protest, NAIDOC has since become a week of celebration. It is a time to acknowledge Aboriginal and Islander culture — past, present and future. Given that it includes such complex and diverse cultures, it is fitting that they be given a week rather than just one day to celebrate.

Can non-Indigenous people be involved in NAIDOC Week?

Aboriginal and Islander people welcome all cultures to participate in their week of celebration. It is an important time for non-Indigenous people to listen and learn about the world's oldest continuous living culture. It is also important that non-Indigenous people understand that the First People of this nation were the first farmers, bakers, navigators, philosophers, astronomers, engineers, artists and explorers. They were not the primitive, stone-age savages they were made out to be by the first Europeans to reach this continent.

OXFORD UNIVERSITY PRESS

Sometimes we can make what we write more interesting to the reader by extending the vocabulary we use.

For example: *I cut the carrots.* We could improve this sentence by simply changing one word.
                    I sliced the carrots. OR *I diced the carrots.*

1 When you read the text on page 96 there may have been words that are unfamiliar to you.

Use the following definitions or synonyms to identify words in the text.

a   an unwelcome takeover of someone else's country ***i***_____

b   avoid, in protest ***b***_____   c   mixed ***d***_____

d   recognise ***a***_____   e   complicated ***c***_____

f   prehistoric ***p***_____

2 Use a dictionary or an online reference to write what the following acronyms stand for.

a   radar _____

b   scuba _____

c   ANZAC _____

d   asap _____

e   FAQ _____

CHALLENGE

Find words for occupations in the text on page 96 that best match these definitions.

a   I paint, draw, sculpt, act, sing or otherwise perform. _____

b   I study the stars and night sky. _____

c   I bake bread, damper, cakes, etc. _____

d   I work the land or tend animals in a way that will produce food, clothing
      or shelter. _____

e   I use the sun, the moon or the stars to find my way. _____

f   I venture into new places to discover what is there. _____

g   I think deeply about why things are the way they are. _____

h   I work out ways to build things and then I build them. _____

BOOK 5: ASSESS YOUR GRAMMAR!

Grammar review

1 Shade the bubble next to the sentence that is correctly punctuated.

- ○ we waited at station pier for the ferry *spirit of tasmania* to arrive
- ○ We waited at station pier for the ferry *spirit of tasmania* to arrive.
- ○ We waited at Station Pier for the ferry, *Spirit of Tasmania* to arrive?
- ○ We waited at Station Pier for the ferry, *Spirit of Tasmania*, to arrive.

2 Shade the bubble next to the sentence that is correctly punctuated.

- ○ "Quickly!" yelled Sam. "Call an ambulance!"
- ○ "Quickly?" yelled Sam. "Call an ambulance?"
- ○ "Quickly yelled Sam! Call an ambulance!"
- ○ Quickly! "yelled Sam." Call an ambulance!

3 Shade the bubble next to the text connective.

The tiger is a carnivore. In other words, the big, stripy cat eats meat!

- ○ The tiger
- ○ is a carnivore
- ○ In other words
- ○ eats meat

4 Shade the bubble next to the correctly punctuated sentence.

- ○ In my lunch box I have an apple a muesli bar a small juice and a sandwich.
- ○ In my lunch, box I have an apple a muesli bar a small juice, and a sandwich.
- ○ In my lunch box I have an apple, a muesli bar, a small juice and a sandwich.
- ○ In my lunch box, I have an apple a muesli bar a small juice, and a sandwich.

5 Shade the bubble next to the subordinating conjunction that would best complete this sentence.

"It is time to take a break, ⬭ there are any more questions," said Mr Lewis.

- ○ since
- ○ unless
- ○ where
- ○ when

OXFORD UNIVERSITY PRESS

6 Shade the bubble next to the word that would best complete this sentence.

The players _____ running out on to the oval.

○ was ○ were ○ is ○ am

7 Shade the bubble next to the word that would best complete this sentence.

They _____ the first to reach the campsite.

○ am ○ was ○ are ○ is

8 Shade the bubble next to the word that would best complete this sentence.

Pat and Pete _____ very clearly.

○ read ○ reads ○ reading ○ reader

9 Write whether the following sentence is past, present or future tense.

We will finish our chores before Mum and Dad get home. _____

10 Write the following as quoted (direct) speech.

The old peasant woman told Merv that the magical horse had taken the road to Cobbleton.

_____

11 Shade the bubble with the prefix that would make **advantage** an antonym.

○ im- ○ in- ○ dis- ○ un-

12 Shade the bubble next to the word that is a homonym for **thrown**.

○ hurled ○ throne ○ caught ○ throwing

HOW AM I DOING?

Tick the boxes if you understand.

Grammar is used to improve and enrich different text types. ☐

Commas can be used to make understanding easier. ☐

Using a wide range of vocabulary makes my writing more interesting and entertaining for the reader. ☐

TIME TO REFLECT

Colour the box when you can do the things listed.

☐ I select specific common, proper, collective, technical or abstract nouns to represent people, places, things and ideas.

☐ I choose suitable nouns to fit the topic of my writing or to represent different characters or settings.

☐ I use a range of adjectives to describe characters and settings.

☐ I know how to expand noun groups with articles and a variety of adjectives for fuller descriptions.

☐ I use thinking and feeling verbs to express opinions.

☐ I use modal verbs like **could, would, should** and **must** to help persuade my audience.

☐ I choose suitable doing, saying or relating verbs to report facts or entertain the reader.

☐ I can use present, past and future tense verbs correctly.

☐ I use adverbs and prepositional phrases to make interesting sentences with details about where, when, how or why something happens.

☐ I use antonyms (opposites) and synonyms (similar meaning) to help describe and compare people, places, things or ideas.

☐ I use paragraphs to organise my writing into logical bundles.

☐ I use topic sentences to introduce the main idea in each paragraph.

☐ I use pronouns that agree with the noun to which they refer. For example: **Evie/she, the boys/they**

☐ I know how to use text connectives to link paragraphs or sentences in time or sequence. For example: **first, then, later, finally**

OXFORD UNIVERSITY PRESS

☐ I sometimes use similes in my writing to describe and compare subjects or to develop a character or setting.

☐ I know how to use coordinating conjunctions (**and, but, so, or**) to make a compound sentence.

☐ I know how to use subordinating conjunctions (for example: *if*, **because**, **until**, **when**) to join a main clause to a subordinate clause.

☐ I know the difference between simple, compound and complex sentences.

☐ I understand that the subject and verb in a sentence must agree.

☐ I recognise how quotation marks are used in quoted (direct) speech.

☐ I understand the difference between quoted (direct) and reported (indirect) speech.

☐ I use commas in lists correctly most of the time.

☐ I understand that an apostrophe of contraction can be used to show where a letter is missing in a shortened word.

☐ I understand how to use an apostrophe of possession.

GLOSSARY

adjective	A word that describes a noun: *red, old, large, round, three*
adverb	A word that usually adds meaning to a verb to tell when, where or how something happened: *slowly, immediately, soon, here* modal adverb (shows degree of certainty): *definitely, probably*
antonym	An opposite: *full/empty, sitting/standing, front/back*
apostrophe of contraction	A punctuation mark that shows where a letter has (or letters have) been omitted: *isn't, we'll, I'm, shouldn't*
apostrophe of possession	A punctuation mark that shows ownership: *Bob's hat, the woman's car, the boys' backpacks*
article	The words *a, an* and *the*
clause	A group of words in a sentence that contain a verb. There are main clauses (*I looked around.*) and subordinate clauses (*when Peter called out*).
comma	A punctuation mark used to separate items in a list, to show a short pause or to separate a main clause and a subordinate clause. *Mum, can I go? When I leave, I will take some apples, bananas, oranges and cherries.*
coordinating conjunction	A joining word used to join two simple sentences or main ideas: *and, but, so, or*
homograph	A word that is spelled the same but has a different meaning: *saw (a tool), saw (past tense of see)*
homonym	A word that looks or sounds the same: *Wind the window out and let the wind in.*
homophone	A word that sounds the same but is spelled differently: *sun/son*
metaphor	A figure of speech that compares something as if it were that thing: *the night was a cloak; the grapefruit moon*
noun	A word that names people, places, animals, things or ideas. Nouns can be: abstract nouns (things that cannot be seen or touched): *happiness, idea* collective nouns (name of groups): *team, flock, bunch, herd*

OXFORD UNIVERSITY PRESS

	common nouns (names of ordinary things): *hat, toys, pet, mouse, clock, bird* concrete nouns (things that can be seen or touched): *book, pet, boy, girl* proper nouns (special names): *Max, Perth, Friday, March, Easter, Australia* technical nouns (sometimes called scientific nouns): *oxygen, larvae*
noun group	A group of words, often including an article, an adjective and a noun, built around a main noun: *the strange, old house*
paragraph	A section of text containing a number of sentences about a particular point. Each paragraph starts on a new line.
phrase	A group of words that adds details about when, where, how, why: *after lunch, with a spoon, for Olivia*
plural	More than one: *chairs, dishes, boxes, cities, donkeys, loaves, fungi*
prefix	A word part that, when added to the beginning of another word or word part, changes the meaning: *dis*appear, *mis*behave
preposition	A word that usually begins a phrase: *on, in, over, under, before*
prepositional phrase	A phrase that starts with a preposition: *in bed, on the weekend*
pronoun	A word that can take the place of a noun to represent a person, place or thing: *he, she, I, it, they, we, us, me, they, them, mine* possessive pronoun: *mine, ours, his, hers, yours, theirs* relative pronoun: *who, whom, whose, which, that*
quoted (direct) speech	The direct speech that someone actually says. Quoted speech uses quotation marks at the start and end of the actual words spoken: *"Recite the three-times table backwards!" the Trunchbull barked.*
reported (indirect) speech	The indirect speech reporting what someone else has said: *The giant told Jack that if he didn't tell him a story then he would gobble him up.*
sentence	A group of words that makes sense and includes a subject and at least one verb. A simple sentence has one main idea and one verb or verb group: *The birds **were sitting** on the fence.* A compound sentence uses *and, but, or, so* to join two main ideas. A compound sentence has two verbs or verb groups: *Some birds **were sitting** on the fence and a cat **was lurking** below.*

	A complex sentence uses subordinate conjunctions to join a main clause with one or more subordinate clauses. A complex sentence has two or more verbs or verb groups: *The tiger snake* **eats** *birds, although frogs* **are** *its preferred prey.*
simile	A figure of speech used to compare two things using the words *like* or *as*: *like a bird, as red as a beetroot*
subject	The noun or noun group naming who or what a sentence is about.
subordinating conjunction	A joining word used to join a main clause and one or more subordinate clauses: *because, since, when, if*
suffix	A word ending. They often change the function of a word: *grace* (abstract noun) – *grace*ful (adjective)
synonym	A word that means the same or nearly the same as another word: *shouts/yells, thin/skinny*
text connective	A signpost word or group of words that tells how the text is developing – generally used to link two sentences or paragraphs: *First, Second, Next, However, For instance*
topic sentence	A sentence, usually placed at the start of a paragraph, that introduces the main point being made in the paragraph.
verb	A word that tells us what is happening in a sentence. Verbs can be: auxiliary verbs (helping verbs used with a main verb): **is** *going,* **could** *go* compound verbs (made up of a helping [auxiliary] and main verb): *is sitting* doing verbs: *walked, swam* modal verbs (telling how sure we are about doing something): *should, could, would, may, might, must, can, will, shall* relating verbs: *am, is, are, had* saying verbs: *said, asked* simple verbs (one word): *went, jump, laughs* thinking and feeling verbs: *know, like*
verb group	A group of words built around a head word that is a verb: *might have been wondering*
verb tense	The form a verb takes to show when an action takes place – in the present, past or future: *runs/is running, thought/was thinking, helps/will help*

OXFORD UNIVERSITY PRESS